Bedford Camper Vans and Motorhomes

The Inside Story

Bedford Camper Vans and Motorhomes

The Inside Story

Martin Watts

The Crowood Press

First published in 2010 by
The Crowood Press Ltd
Ramsbury, Marlborough
Wiltshire SN8 2HR

www.crowood.com

British Library Cataloguing-in-Publication Data
A catalogue record for this book is available from the British Library.

ISBN 978 1 84797 157 9

Typeset and designed by D & N Publishing
Baydon, Wiltshire.

Printed and bound in Malaysia by Times Offset (M) Sdn Bhd.

contents

introduction

The Bedford name is one that is synonymous with quality, robust commercial vehicles. First introduced in 1931, Bedford was the brand name given to Vauxhall's commercial division, and the name of the vehicle marque was derived from the county in which these vehicles were constructed: Bedfordshire, England. In a twenty-year period from its inception, Bedford went from strength to strength, attaining excellent sales and an enviable reputation for its range of commercial vehicles. During the Second World War Bedford vehicles were in demand by the military, and the formidable Churchill tanks were also built at the factory for use by the British Army.

The aim of this book is to concentrate on the Bedford vehicles that were utilized for conversion to camper vans and motorhomes, and therefore we need to jump forward to 1952 as being a significant milestone in Bedford history, certainly in terms of British-built camper vans. That heralded the introduction of the Bedford CA light van range, a vehicle which was to become such a familiar sight in Britain over the next sixteen years. During that time the external design of the CA altered little, apart from cosmetic changes to the size of the windscreen and the wheels, and it was seen in every guise from the basic delivery van, to the pick-up and mobile shop to the minibus. But despite the vehicle's success as an everyday utility base, the Bedford CA will be forever associated with Martin Walter Ltd and its Dormobile Caravan conversion, a model which introduced thousands of British residents to the joys of motorcaravanning. By 1969 the CA range had become somewhat dated and Vauxhall Motors released their all-new model, the CF range. Whereas the previous CA vans had really been utilized only by Martin Walter Ltd for conversion to camper vans, the new CF was far more appealing to the conversion companies due to its increased dimensions and uprated mechanical components. Within its first year of production more camper van models were introduced using the CF chassis than all those released in the seventeen-years production of the CA. Year by year, more CF-based camper vans were unveiled, and, as time went on, the CF was upgraded and modified by Vauxhall Motors, making it more and more attractive to

ABOVE: Fans and enthusiasts of Bedford-based camper vans and motorhomes will be aware that the whole wonderful affair began with the famous CA by Bedford. That unmistakable shape and familiar driving cab with sliding doors are held in great affection to this day. The example seen here is the revised model from 1959.

LEFT: The camper vans and motorhomes produced by Martin Walter Ltd of Folkestone became such an everyday sight on British roads during the 1950s and 1960s that people began to refer to all such motorized camping models as Dormobiles when, in fact, only Martin Walter produced a genuine Dormobile motorcaravan. The model seen here is the all-GRP bodied Bedford Debonair motorhome, a revolutionary model for 1964.

both new and established motorcaravanners. In addition to the success that the CF was enjoying in Britain, it was also proving to be a popular campervan base in many European countries.

During its eighteen-years production run, the CF light commercial range underwent several design changes until full-time production came to an end in 1987. Between 1969 and 1987 the CF was constantly in the top five of the favoured base vehicles used for conversion to camper van and motorhome by the leisure industry. It is therefore not surprising that, due to the numbers converted and the fact that it remained in production until 1987, so many Bedford CF-based camper vans have survived to this day.

Although 1987 did see the end of the once-great Bedford marque in its familiar guise as a market leader, it was not quite the end of Bedford's involvement with the motorcaravan industry. The Vauxhall/Bedford Midi range was unveiled in the mid 1980s, although it was not a great commercial success and was certainly not held in the same regard as the previous CA and CF ranges. Despite a handful of conversion companies using the Midi as a camper-van base, it failed to capture the imagination of the motorcaravan buyers and only the Auto-Sleeper Midi, Devon models and Midi-Home by Autohomes were conversions of note.

By 1986 there had been a reorganization of the Bedford marque and a joint venture with Isuzu led to the formation of IBC Vehicles. In 1986 the Bedford Rascal was introduced, which, in

ABOVE: *The term Dormobile will probably conjure up this iconic image, the cute Bedford CA transformed into the Dormobile Caravan with pram hood-style rising roof; this 1958 example was lovingly restored by Bedford enthusiast Alan Kirtley.*

LEFT: *Many motorists were saddened to see the demise of the CA range in 1969, but the new CF van quickly gained many fans, especially as a camper van. Part of the CF assembly is seen here in the Luton factory.*

Any book that delves into the history of Bedford camper vans and motorhomes would not be complete without a mention of the hugely popular Bedford HA light van. In production for many years, the HA gained favour as a camper van only after Martin Walter gave it their full Dormobile treatment and released the Dormobile Roma. An early Mk.I model is seen here, owned by Sean Browes and currently (2009) being restored.

effect, was a restyled Suzuki Supercarry, fitted with the diminutive 970cc petrol engine. Whereas the larger Midi van failed to attract the attention of the major motorcaravan converters, the Rascal, on the other hand, was used to great effect by the giant Autohomes business in Dorset. This company used the Rascal pick-up version as a base for a micro coach-built camper, the Bedford Bambi. Through the remainder of the 1980s, the little Bambi really did become a great sales success, winning several prizes in the leisure industry. The British caravan builders Elddis also utilized the Rascal pick-up, and entered the micro-camper sector with their own Elddis Nipper. One would not have thought that the Bedford Rascal offered dimensions of adequate proportions in its basic panel-van format, but the Danbury motorcaravan converters went on to release their tiny Danbury Renegade with its miniature rising roof and diminutive interior fitments.

The demise of the Rascal range in the early 1990s brought to a close several decades of Bedford use in the camper van/motorhome market, much to the chagrin of the marque's dedicated followers. In 1998 GM and Isuzu ended their joint building venture, and from that moment the factory operated as GMM Luton. That famous griffin badge, which adorned so many Bedford vehicles, could be seen once again on the bonnet (hood) of such light commercial models as the Vauxhall Vivaro and the Vauxhall Movano, although only a few bespoke converters have used these vans for conversion to camper vans.

Despite the loss of the Bedford name/brand, it is a marque that will live long in the memory of commercial vehicle enthusiasts around the world. My hope is that this book will act as a reference source for all owners, fans and enthusiasts of Bedford camper vans, in Britain and in all the corners of the world where the Bedford was exported. It was not possible to write a chapter on every model of Bedford camper built over the years, there were simply too many. I have therefore offered descriptions of the more popular models and of some of the unusual examples.

Bedford CF camper vans and motorhomes have a tremendous following today, despite the fact that the last CF was built in 1987. There are large numbers still in use and being enjoyed by their owners; this pair of CF models was on display at a classic vehicle show – green/white CI Autohome/Motorhome (foreground) and the beige/white Advantura.

1

Vauxhall-Bedford history

The Vauxhall Motors story began in 1857 when Alexander Wilson started his engineering company in Vauxhall, London. He later built marine engines and other ancillaries and by 1903 the first motor car had been produced. In 1905 the company was moved from London to Luton, and Vauxhall Motors was formed in 1907. This picture shows an early view of the Luton factory premises with staff and two Vauxhall cars.

The original Vauxhall company was founded by Alexander Wilson in the Vauxhall area of London in 1857, although the name of the company at that time was Alex Wilson and Co. It was involved with the manufacture of marine engines and pumps and did not build its first motor car until 1903. As the development and popularity of the motor car increased, the company made the decision to move from London to a purpose-built factory at Luton in Bedfordshire around 1905. That original factory covered a land area of around 1½ acres (0.60ha), which was to increase to around 40 acres (16.20ha) by the 1930s. By the time the company had moved to Luton it was trading under the name Vauxhall Iron Works but, with the increased production of motor vehicles, it was renamed as Vauxhall Motors.

The Vauxhall emblem, which has adorned so many vehicles over the years, is one of the most famous in British motoring history and features the griffin. The emblem was derived from the coat of arms of Faulke de Breaute, a soldier who was granted the Manor of Luton in the thirteenth century for his services to King John, and his house, Fulks Hall, eventually became Vaux Hall and then Vauxhall. The griffin emblem, still used by Vauxhall Motors today, has been redesigned nine times since the 1920s.

During the very early part of the twentieth century Vauxhall Motors concentrated its design and build efforts on family cars, quickly gaining a reputation for reliability and build quality. The popularity of the marque during this time came to the attention of General Motors in the United Sates, and by 1925 Vauxhall had been purchased by GM for the sum of $2.5 million. By this time in Vauxhall's history its commercial vehicles were branded as Chevrolet-Bedford to reflect GM's ownership, but in 1925 the commercial arm of Vauxhall Motors became Bedford. In 1931 the first Bedford appeared, a 2-ton lorry (truck) similar to the Chevrolet-Bedford LQ, and then by 1932 a 15cwt lorry and a 12cwt light delivery van had been added to the Bedford line-up. Soon after came the 8cwt vans, the ASYC and the ASXC, this AS range being a derivative of the Light Six car; the AS range continued until 1939. In 1933 came yet more new Bedford models: the 3-ton range, known as the WT series, consisting of an SWB (WTH) and an LWB (WLG), with a further derivative given the initials WTL. As the 1930s unfolded there was no stopping this fast developing Bedford brand, with new models being released in order to fill a niche in the commercial vehicle market. By the mid 1930s Bedford sales accounted for around 40 per cent of the British market in the 30cwt category and 45 per cent of the small bus sector. Bedford were also able to boast of 63 per cent of British lorry exports. In 1935 the WTB bus chassis was unveiled, quickly followed in 1938 by the introduction of the HC light van range, this being based on the Vauxhall Ten motor car. The 1930s, the first decade of the Bedford brand, had certainly proved to be a huge success as by 1937 the 30,000th commercial vehicle had been built bearing the Bedford badge. The Bedford bandwagon was certainly in full spate during this period with the Vauxhall public relations department boasting, quite rightly, that there was a Bedford for every situation, from heavy haulage to light deliveries, and from refuse trucks to passenger-carrying buses and coaches. The future looked bright indeed for a marque still in its infancy. And then came the war.

The contribution to the war effort made by the Bedford marque can be summed up swiftly in the one word 'immense', and although a full historical account of the Bedford vehicle role in the war falls outside the remit of a book dealing essentially with motorcaravans, it would be remiss not give an overview of the part that this great vehicle brand did play.

Bedford had begun to develop a 15cwt truck in 1935 for the British armed forces, and this finally entered service in 1939 as the MW. This truck became one of the most versatile base vehicles of the period and was put to use as a personnel carrier, fuel tanker, water

The Vauxhall/Bedford plant in Luton did not escape the ravages of bombing during the Second World War. On 30 August 1940 the factory took a direct hit and thirty-nine employees were killed and many more seriously injured. Vauxhall Motors made a significant contribution to the war effort, building over 250,000 Bedford trucks, armour-piercing shells and 5 million jerricans; in addition they also did most of the work on the first twelve jet aircraft engines.

tanker, delivery truck and anti-aircraft gun carrier. By the end of the war in 1945 close to 70,000 examples of the MW truck had been built.

In 1939 the Bedford lorries in the K, the M and the O series were given a make-over for military use, mostly in their styling with alterations to the bonnet and the front headlights. These military models were then redesignated as the OX and the OY series and were put to use covering a wide spectrum of tasks, most notably as tankers, for

general deliveries, as mobile canteens and the Tasker semi-trailer for the RAF. At the same time a large number of the OXD 1.5 ton chassis were also converted in order to make the Bedford OXA armoured vehicles, and in excess of 70,000 OY and OX vehicles were produced. Entering service in 1941, the four-wheel drive, forward control QL was given the nickname 'Queen Lizzie' by military personnel. The QL model was yet another Bedford that would be put to a variety of uses and lead to the development of a further model, the QLD, which was mostly used as a troop carrier. It is worth noting that many of the Bedford QL series were still being used by the British armed forces well into the 1960s.

One of the most impressive feats achieved by Vauxhall Motors during the war years concerned the design, development and building of the Churchill tank. The company was given the task of building, completely from scratch, a tank in under a year. The massive, 38-ton Churchill tank went from being an idea to a full working model in less than twelve months, and a total of 5,640 were built at Luton and at other plants, supplied with parts from Vauxhall HQ. No fewer than six different prototypes of Vauxhall-built tanks were under test by the time the war came to an end. In addition to the 250,000 Bedford vehicles that

The most impressive output of the war at Luton was the building of over 5,600 Churchill tanks. This rare picture was taken by Arthur Akers on D-Day+1 while he was serving with the Royal Engineers, and shows a Churchill tank being unloaded from an LST.

Larger Loads....
Longer Life....
Lower Costs....

The New

BEDFORD 10/12 *cwt. Van*

DESIGNED TO DO A VAN'S JOB BETTER

LEFT: The most significant year in Vauxhall Motors' history with regard to motorcaravans was 1952. This saw the introduction of the Bedford CA range, a light commercial van that would leave an indelible mark upon the history of both British and European motoring. Martin Walter Ltd of Folkestone immediately set about transforming the basic CA van into a general utility vehicle with passenger-carrying seats and side windows, and from that moment on, the famous Bedford Dormobile was born.

Vauxhall Motors had produced for the military, they also manufactured 5 million jerrycans, helmets, and armour-piercing shells for 6-pounder guns. Over 90 per cent of the work on the first twelve British jet engines was also completed by Vauxhall. Given the total contribution to the war effort by Vauxhall Motors, no one can say that the 12,000 members of staff did not play their part. The Germans were obviously aware of the work taking place at the Vauxhall plant because on 30 August 1940 the factory was subjected to a heavy air raid, and thirty-nine employees were killed with a further forty seriously injured. Damage to the factory was considerable, and yet it was producing vehicles there again just six days later.

Once the war was over, production continued apace at the Luton factory on both family saloons and Bedford commercial vehicles. Car manufacture resumed on the H-, I- and J-type cars and on the K, M and O series Bedford commercials. By 1947 the 500,000th Bedford truck had been built, and by 1948 a £14 million expansion of the Luton plant had begun. But the year which will be of great interest to enthusiasts of Bedford-based motorcaravans is, as we noted earlier, 1952, for it was then that the David Jones-designed Bedford CA light van was introduced. It was a vehicle that would not only change the face of light commercial vehicle usage in Britain, but it would also be the base vehicle used by Martin Walter Ltd of Folkestone to launch their Dormobile Caravan.

In the following year, 1953, Vauxhall Motors celebrated the Jubilee of the Vauxhall motor car; this year also saw the Bedford K, L and M range replaced by the new A-series. As the decade unfurled, Vauxhall Motors forged ahead by announcing a £36 million expansion

By 1957 Martin Walter had introduced their first fully-fitted Dormobile camper van with interior fitments such as a cooker and sink. This 1958 model has been full restored and clearly shows the small rising roof and the rear port-hole window, both trademarks of the early Dormobile examples. This particular model became synonymous with 1950s outdoor living and introduced thousands to the joys of motorcaravanning.

project in 1954, closely followed by the transfer of Bedford vehicle production to the Dunstable plant. Notable milestones in the history of the company quickly followed, and by 1958 the millionth Bedford had been built. As the 1950s drew to a close the company released the news that it had built the two-millionth Vauxhall car, and in 1959 a new car plant at Ellesmere Port was announced. Vauxhall Motors launched a huge sales drive initiative in that year in the form of a Bedford convoy under the heading 'The Bedford Trans-Europe Caravan' (the word caravan being used to describe the convoy, not a camping vehicle). This convoy contained fourteen Bedford vehicles of varying type, from a passenger-carrying coach to an ambulance, and a tipper truck to a Dormobile camper van. The convoy was a huge sales drive through eleven

countries, which began in Portugal and finished 10,000 miles later in Finland. It took six months to complete, and the vehicles stopped off in 190 towns and cities en route, with drivers supplied by General Motors outlets in the several countries. The sales convoy obviously had the desired effect because the following year the sales of Bedford commercial vehicles escalated in the countries visited.

The next significant new vehicle release of interest to camper-van enthusiasts came in 1964 when Vauxhall unveiled the Bedford HA 6/8cwt light van. This vehicle would form the basis for the Dormobile Roma, a compact camper with ending tailgate and small rising roof. The 1960s were a time of rapid new releases of Vauxhall vehicles, with the FB Victor coming in 1961, the HA Viva in 1963 and the Ventora in

Maurice Calthorpe was the first to offer a coach-built motorhome example on the CA chassis, though it still retained his famous curved rising roof. This early publicity picture for the Calthorpe Bedford dates from 1957 and was taken in central London.

1968. But as the swinging sixties finished so did production of the Bedford CA, which had been so popular since its introduction in 1952. Replacing the CA range in 1969 was the CF Bedford, a vehicle that was to figure so prominently in the world of motorcaravanning for the next eighteen years. That was also a year that marked a significant milestone for the Vauxhall Motors Bedford brand as it was announced that the

two-millionth Bedford vehicle had been produced. With regard to the heavier Bedford commercials at this time, the TK model was used in just about every form throughout the 1960s and the 1970s, from fire tender to military vehicle, and from horse box to flatbed truck. The Bedford RL model, made famous as the 'Green Goddess' emergency fire vehicle in Britain, continued in production until 1969 and was still in

use around the world well into the present century, which itself says quite a lot about Bedford dependability.

The 1970s were another decade of growth for Vauxhall Motors and began with the release of the HC Viva and the Bedford M-type 4×4 in 1970. Further releases during the decade included the Vauxhall FE, Magnum, Bedford TM, Chevette, Chevanne, Cavalier, Carlton and Astra. The Bedford CF was to establish itself as a firm favourite in the motor-caravan market throughout the 1970s, both in Britain and on the Continent (where it was sold as the Opel Blitz). Bedford vehicles were being assembled in twenty countries around the world by 1975 as it was more economic to export parts than entire vehicles.

In each decade Vauxhall Motors were able to announce further milestones. With the fiftieth anniversary of the Bedford marque under their belts by 1981, the following year saw the 1.5 millionth Bedford exported. By 1984 the Astra van and the Midi van had been launched and GM invested £100 million in car manufacturing facilities. The theme of further investment is a recurring one throughout the 1980s with £90 million invested in a new paint facility at Luton

The Bedford CA model was constantly modified during its long production run and this picture clearly illustrates the first one-piece windscreen, which replaced the original 'split' windscreen design. On the left is a Dormobile and on the right is a Calthorpe Home-Cruiser.

The innovative Dormobile Debonair model was launched in 1964 on the CA chassis. With the exception of the front nose section, this was an all-GRP-bodied camper with a spacious interior and rear-end dinette. It was one of only a handful of coach-built motorhomes produced using the CA chassis; the Debonair body was later carried over to the CF on its introduction in 1969.

By the mid 1960s the CA had undergone more design changes, the most notable of which was the much larger windscreen, as seen on this publicity shot for the Dormobile Romany De Luxe model.

ABOVE: The CA range gave way to the CF range in 1969 and immediately the converters set to work designing and producing CF, camper van and motorhome examples. One of the most successful camper van models produced on the CF throughout the 1970s and the 1980s was the Auto-Sleeper rising roof, seen here.

LEFT: Competing for the title of 'best selling CF camper' during the 1970s was the Dormobile Freeway, seen here at a classic vehicle show. It featured the famous candy-stripe Dormobile rising roof and integrated front luggage rack in fibreglass.

in 1985 and £50 million in the modernization of the Luton plant in 1989. The year 1987 would witness the passing of the hugely popular Bedford CF, which was then discontinued. If the company's management expected the newly released 1 ton Midi to fill the void left by the CF they were sadly mistaken. Specifically, the Midi did not fit the criteria too well for conversion to motorcaravan and, as a result, only two converters of note (in Britain) offered camper van models on the Midi.

But a decision made by the company in 1983 would have a prolonged effect on commercial vehicle manufacture in Luton. In that year, Bedford, which was by then part of the GM Overseas Commercial Vehicle Corporation, became the Bedford Commercial Vehicle Division. Although this did not sound like a significant press release to many, it did, in fact, signal the beginning of the end for the Bedford marque as a 'standalone' brand. By the mid 1980s GM had entered into a partnership with Isuzu Motors of Japan in order to form IBC (Isuzu, Bedford Commercials), and this alliance initially produced the Midi van and the Bedford Rascal. The military

sector of Bedford was hived off to the AWD Company around 1986. To the diehard enthusiasts, this was really the end of 'real' Bedford vans, though one could not argue that the diminutive Rascal van (and pick-up) were a huge sales success. In the motorcaravan industry the Bedford Rascal was put to good use as the base for the very popular Autohomes Bambi, a compact, coach-built model ideal for a couple. Elddis also produced their own miniature coach-built camper, the Nipper, again based on the small dimensions of the Rascal, with the established British

This home conversion was seen touring around New Zealand some years ago. Constructed entirely from wood with a rear entrance door it really does look the part mated to a Bedford J-series chassis. The J series was not used for British production motorhomes but was commonly used for self-build prototypes in several countries.

ABOVE: The hugely popular Bedford CF enjoyed a long production run between 1969 and 1987, and was subjected to several design changes along the way. Seen here is an Auto-Sleeper Clubman model, dating from the mid 1980s, and still sought after today on the classic scene.

RIGHT: Purists might argue that the diminutive Rascal model was not a true Bedford due to its Japanese origins, but it did carry the Bedford logo and it was built in Britain. This is the Bambi by Autohomes, a very small, coach-built model based on the Rascal pick-up, an ideal two-person camper van with the ability to sleep a child in the over-cab area. The Bambi model has a very enthusiastic following, a dedicated owners' club and good spares availability.

converter Danbury offering a panel van model with rising roof, sold under the name of the Renegade.

The IBC/GM joint venture remained until the mid 1990s when GM took over the full ownership of IBC Vehicles. They immediately announced that they would increase employment by 40 per cent at Luton in the years ahead due to the development of a new medium van, to be produced in conjunction with Renault. This joint venture would result in the production of the Renault Trafic (also sold as the Vauxhall Vivaro and Nissan Primastar) and the larger Renault Master (also sold as the Vauxhall Movano).

In 2000 Vauxhall announced that car production was to cease at Luton and, despite the many meetings and demonstrations that followed this news, car production ended in 2003. Incidentally, this would be just two years short of the magical one-hundred years-production milestone for car building by Vauxhall at Luton (they celebrated their ninetieth year in 1995). In spite of this, that famous griffin logo would still adorn the front grille of vehicles built at Luton, but the vehicles were now vans and not cars, and Vauxhall vans not Bedfords. That IBC/Renault joint venture has gone from strength to strength, and in 2003 the Vauxhall Vivaro won the award for the 'best small van' for the second year

Introduced in 1985, the Midi, like the Rascal, was a joint Isuzu/Bedford venture fitted with a range of Isuzu engine options. The Midi failed to establish itself as an ideal base for camper van conversion, with only Auto-Sleepers, Autohomes and Devon producing models of note. Early Midi models were badged as Bedford and later versions as Vauxhall.

in succession and by 2006 the 400,000th Vivaro had been built. For some reason the motorcaravan converters have overlooked both the Vivaro and the Movano as bases for camper van conversion; this is a mystery since both vehicles lend themselves very well for this purpose. It has fallen to the DIY brigade of camper-van enthusiasts to convert the Movano in particular, because in high-top form it makes the perfect camper van base.

Luton was really built on the success of the Vauxhall plant over the years, it was a huge employer and the scars left by the car plant's closure will take some time to heal. Most of the old car production site has now been cleared, but a tenuous link remains between the old Bedford vehicles and modern-day production there. The old AA factory block where Bedford CF assembly took place became home to the griffin-badged Vivaro/Movano vans.

Bringing the Vauxhall/Bedford camper van story into the present century is the Vauxhall Vivaro, and in basic van form it has proved to be a top-selling light commercial, picking up several awards. The model seen here is the high-top Vivaro Highlander produced by Mill Garage in Scotland.

An artist's impression from a period Vauxhall Motors sales brochure showing the various uses for the Bedford CA chassis: this picture depicts the CA pick-up, milk float and Dormobile Caravan, but in addition there were mobile shops, minibuses, gown vans, removal vans and general delivery vans.

2

Bedford – base vehicles

BEDFORD CA

The CA light commercial range was released by Vauxhall Motors in April of 1952 and the payload forms were 10/12cwt, with a 15cwt model to follow in 1958. The CA range, in varying forms, became a hugely popular sight on UK roads enjoying a seventeen-year production, which was brought to a close by the release of the CF range in 1969.

The Bedford CA was a model that was constantly updated throughout its production run, the most noticeable

external modification being the windscreen size. When released in 1952 the CA was fitted with a two-piece 'split screen', this was replaced by a one-piece screen in 1959, together with a redesigned front grille. The windscreen was widened again by June of the same year; it would remain at this size until 1964 when it was increased again in both height and width. As far as the power plant was concerned, the CA began with a 1508cc petrol unit (1952–63), which, in turn, was replaced by a larger 1595cc engine from 1963. Two diesel

engines were offered as options during the CA's production, these were, first, the Perkins 4.99 (from June 1961) and from 1965 onwards the Perkins 4.108. The wheels fitted to the CA were altered during production, beginning with 16in upon its release, changing to 15in in 1957. By 1960 the sizes were changed once again when the smaller, 13in examples were fitted. These are the more obvious changes and modifications made constantly throughout the vehicle's life, but the biggest of these changes came in 1964 when the Mk.II

RIGHT: A period black-and-white illustration showing the underside of the Bedford CA chassis, with the rear axle, exhaust system and front steering gear all clearly visible.

BELOW: The Bedford HA was the light van version of the Vauxhall Viva car, a van which became popular throughout the 1960s and the 1970s, not least with the Post Office, which purchased around 33,000 of them between 1972 and 1982. As a camper van it was converted only by Dormobile, when it became the Roma, a compact model with a rising roof.

version was announced (although it was not introduced until May 1965). All CA variants featured a 3/4 speed column-mounted gear change. The CA range was discontinued in 1969 when the all-new Bedford CF range was introduced.

The CA, despite being a popular delivery vehicle, gained such an excellent reputation within motorcaravanning only through the Dormobile conversions. Despite the appearance of other conversions such as the Hadrian, the Calthorpe, the Pegasus and the Bedmobile, the CA will be forever associated with the great Folkestone company of Martin Walter Ltd (Dormobile).

BEDFORD CF

As we saw, the CF model was a direct replacement for the extremely successful CA. Initially the CF range used the 1599cc and the 1975cc petrol engine, with the Perkins 1760cc being the diesel option. By 1972 the petrol-engine sizes had been increased to 1759cc and

2279cc. The engine position in the CF remained similar to that in the old CA model, being mounted half in the cab and half under the front bonnet, in true 'forward-control' fashion. The option of sliding cab doors (as seen on the earlier CA) was again available on the CF range, though this feature on the CF in particular was more popular on goods delivery vans than on those converted into motorcaravans.

Most motorcaravans were built on either the CF220 or the CF250 base, these numbers representing the gross vehicle weight (GVW); for example, the 220 meant 2.20 tons. The designation badge was carried on the front wheel arch. The majority of motorcaravans were based on the single rear wheel CF bases, some of the later, much larger coach-built examples using the twin rear wheelbase.

The CF range continued to undergo minor alterations and modifications until 1980, when the CF was given a facelift. A plastic front grille was the most noticeable external change; the range was also modified and consisted of the CF230, the 250, the 280 and the 350. This revamped model is often incorrectly referred to as the CF2, but in fact the official CF2 was not introduced until 1984. The CF production run ended in 1987 having enjoyed an even longer eighteen-year span.

BEDFORD/VAUXHALL MIDI

Brought in as a replacement for the CF van, the Midi was a Japanese design with an Isuzu power plant. It had obviously been decided by this time that it was financially more viable to enter into a joint manufacturing partnership with another vehicle producer. Production of the Midi began during the mid 1980s and was available in Britain only until 1994.

The engines fitted to the Midi ranged from 1.8 or 2.0ltr petrol, and diesel options of 2.0, 2.2 and 2.4ltr. An up-market people carrier was also launched under the name of the Albany. The only three conversions of note carried out by British converters on the Midi van were the Midi-Home by Autohomes and the Auto-Sleeper model; Devon conversions also fitted out the Midi as camper vans, the Dove and the Domino model.

BEDFORD/VAUXHALL RASCAL

Produced between 1986 and 1993, the Bedford Rascal was, in fact, based on the Japanese Suzuki Carry. Very small and compact in size, it quickly gained an enthusiastic following. Easy to park, with a good load-carrying space, good economy and easily manoeuvrable in tight spaces, the Rascal established

ABOVE: Many loyal followers mourned the passing of the Bedford CA range when it was replaced by the CF in 1969. As a base for conversion to camper van and motorhome, the CF became one of the most popular base vehicles of the 1970s and 1980s and retains many admirers to this day, unsurprising as so many good examples have survived. Pictured here is the Bedford Bedouin by CI Autohomes of Poole, available in only one colour, sandy/gold to reflect the Bedouin theme, a hugely popular model in the 1970s.

RIGHT: IBC (Isuzu, Bedford Commercials) was formed at Luton in the mid 1980s and signalled the end of the Bedford brand in its own right. As a result of the Isuzu partnership, the Bedford Rascal and the larger Bedford Midi were launched (both were rebadged as Vauxhalls later). Given its diminutive size, good economy and ease of handling, the Rascal proved very popular as a delivery van and a pick-up. Despite its tiny interior proportions it was converted to a camper van by several companies including Autohomes, Elddis and Danbury. The rising-roof model seen here is a bespoke conversion.

itself with a wide variety of tradesmen. The Rascal was available not only as a panel van with side loading doors and rear tailgate, but also in pick-up form. The engine power came from the 970cc Suzuki petrol unit situated under the front cab floor. For the purposes of motorcaravan design and conversion, the Rascal was used by Autohomes as the Bedford Bambi, Elddis as the Nipper and Danbury as the Renegade. Despite being out of production for many years, the Rascal still has a loyal following.

The Rascal was sold around the world under several names: in India it was the Maruti Omni, in Korea it became the Daewoo Labo/Damas, Australians knew it as the Holden Scurry and in France it carried the delightful name, Chatenet Yak. From 1990 the Bedford grille badge was replaced by the Vauxhall lettering.

As far as camper vans and motorhomes are concerned, the Bedford name died with the Rascal and the Midi, but it was by no means the end of the famous griffin badge in the world of motorcaravanning. The griffin logo entered the present century of outdoor leisure adorning the Vauxhall Movano and Vivaro vans. Sadly, none of the mainstream British converters use these models, but they have found favour with the smaller concerns offering limited run production and custom-built camper vans. Seen here is the rear view of the Movano Highlander by Mill Garage of Scotland, a well converted camper van offering full internal standing height.

3 *Dormobile Caravan* (Bedford CA)

One of the most iconic images of camper vans from a bygone era, the Bedford Dormobile, the model that brought motorcaravanning to the masses. This publicity picture dates from 1959 and was issued by Martin Walter Ltd. The company always used Folkestone beauty spots for their photographic locations, and no doubt these ladies were either company employees or partners of the directors. This particular Dormobile is fitted with the larger roof and would have had two single bunk beds installed. Note also the lack of any trademark Dormobile vehicle side flashes; these early models relied on two-tone paintwork with a thin painted coach line around the waistline.

Alongside the Volkswagen 'splitty', this was quite possibly the prime model from the classic years of British motorcaravanning, which conjures up such an iconic image of outdoor leisure days from the past. That candy-stripe canvas roof, hinged high in the air from one side, was such a popular sight on campsites around Britain during the 1950s and the 1960s, and I am, of course, referring to the famous patented Dormobile rising roof, as fitted to many Dormobile models from the mid 1950s. In the raised position one knew instantly, even from a great distance, that it must be a 'Dormobile' (although it was used under licence by a couple of other converters). Although it was not the first rising roof to be fitted to a conversion (that honour going to Maurice Calthorpe), it certainly became the enduring image of 1950s and 1960s campsites around Britain.

Martin Walter Ltd first fitted their side-hinged rising roof to the Bedford CA conversion in 1957 and marketed this utility vehicle as the 'Dormobile Caravan'. This vehicle propelled the Folkestone company into becoming the leading conversion specialist in the UK motorcaravan world. The overnight success of the Dormobile Caravan on the CA remains one of the great vehicle sales success stories of the twentieth century. It was a case of the right product at the right time: in the mid-1950s, just over a decade after the end of the Second World War, the UK public was starting to warm to the joys of motorcaravanning and the Dormobile Caravan ticked all the correct boxes, including affordability. Until the release of this model, it had been trailer caravans (tourers) that had won the hearts of the public when it came to enjoying the outdoor life, but that now

began to change, and much of that change was down to Martin Walter Ltd.

The Dormobile Caravan was exhibited at various motor shows, and test models were loaned to leading car publications for both long- and short-term tests. The resulting publicity was good, to say the least, for Martin Walter's sales, and the Dormobile legend was born. A handful of those very early examples thankfully still survive on the CA chassis.

To this day, those early models remain pleasing to look at with their round porthole window in the side and the early version of that famous rising roof. Throughout the late 1950s the company kept the price of this model to an absolute minimum in order to maximize sales; it was one of the lowest priced models on the annual listings/buyers guides. In 1958 (in standard form) the cost of a Dormobile Caravan was £725, beating the two nearest rivals

21

Dormobile Caravan (Bedford CA)

ABOVE: The more familiar Bedford Dormobile model, which we all came to know and love during the 1960s. This well kept example is owned by Tony Hall, a dedicated classic vehicle enthusiast and classic camper van lover. This is the De Luxe model with rear louvred windows, integrated front luggage rack and the distinctive fibreglass side mouldings.

LEFT: A rear corner shot of the Dormobile Romany with the rising roof in the fully raised position. The attention to detail by Martin Walter Ltd when it came to the external design features of this model was quite superb, and it was though the Bedford CA was first conceived simply to become the 'Dormobile'.

Rear view of the Romany De Luxe model, which shows quite clearly the fibreglass moulding applied by Martin Walter Ltd to the side of the bodywork; note the absence of the rubber infill in the aluminium extrusion; this is the next part of the restoration to be undertaken by Tony Hall.

the Calthorpe Home-Cruiser and Pitt Moto-Caravan by some margin. The giant Martin Walter concern did, of course, have a head start on their rivals during the 1950s, they were already very well established coachbuilders, had huge factory premises and a trained workforce. Add to these factors their long-standing relationship with Vauxhall Motors and you have a recipe for undoubted success, as long as you have the goods to market in the first instance, and they certainly did. In terms of sales the Dormobile Caravan left all other British models trailing in its wake; it really was in a league of its own. In fact, such was the demand for Martin Walter Bedford CA conversions (both the Utility van and the Dormobile Caravan) that base vehicles were transported by a direct rail link from Luton to the Martin Walter factory in Folkestone. One figure certainly worth noting here concerns the Bedford CA conversion by the company in 1959: by that year alone they produced 10,000 Bedford CA conversions, which included the Dormobile Caravan, the Utilabrake, the Utilicon, the Utilabus and the Workobus.

At the start of the 1960s, the famous Dormobile rising roof was enlarged and the Dormobile Caravan was now the Romany. By the time the company had put on its display at that year's Motor Show, the model line-up numbered fifteen examples on six different base vehicles. But despite extending their range of models it remained the Romany that was the most favoured by the buyers. The Romany range actually comprised five different options: first, the Romany Standard; this was a Bedford CAS (short wheelbase model) with a fixed factory metal roof. Next came the Romany Super, again on the Bedford CAS model, but this time fitted with a rising roof. These two models were then duplicated, but this time on the Bedford CAL (long wheelbase model). The top of the Romany range was the De Luxe, also based on the Bedford CAL; this model had both a rising

Interior of the Romany as seen through the twin opening rear doors, with the driver's side seats folded flat to create either a single bed or a bench-style seat. On the opposite side the rear single seat and the front passenger seat are arranged around the table for dining. The Dormatic seats in this model retain their original 1960s Dormobile upholstery in light green vinyl.

To the rear (passenger side) are the kitchen facilities, basic yet functional with a two-burner gas hob and grill, and plastic sink alongside. The hand water pump can be seen between the sink and the hob, with a small cutlery drawer below and further storage space in the main kitchen unit behind sliding doors.

roof and a roof rack built on to the frontal roof area. This gave a very sleek and streamlined appearance. Adding to the attractive external appearance of the De Luxe model were the GRP tail fins fitted on the rear sides of the vehicle. This Romany range, in 1964, stretched in price from £658 for the Standard through to £888 for the De Luxe. As if this Romany range was not confusing enough, another Bedford CA model was offered at £995, this was the Deauville. It had most of the features found in and on the De Luxe offering, but the interior was finished in real wood, as opposed to the laminate-faced cupboards of the other models.

Throughout the 1960s the Dormobile Romany continued to be the biggest selling panel-van conversion in the country. The model name was eventually carried over to the Bedford CF when it replaced the CA in 1969.

For the purposes of description I shall concentrate on the Bedford CA Romany from the late 1960s, as by this time it had undergone considerable changes from the early example. The Romany was a four-door model featuring sliding cab doors and twin opening rear doors, and with the exception of the Dormatic seats and their variable positioning, the interior was of the traditional, panel-van layout. Looking toward the cab from the rear, there was a kitchen on the left fitted with a sink, two-burner hob with grill, draw and storage cupboards below. A water carrier was situated on the end, nearest the rear doors, and this supplied water to the sink via a hand pump. On the opposite side from the kitchen were a wardrobe and a further storage unit. The base of the wardrobe incorporated a pull-out stool/seat for use when cooking. All units in the Romany Standard and Super models were of a light wood-effect laminate. Fitted along the vehicle

Opposite the kitchen is the wardrobe and chest of drawers for clothes storage, and at the base of the wardrobe is the trademark pull-out stool/step. This neat device was designed to act as a stool for the cook when in the kitchen and as a stepping stool for access to the upper bunk beds in the rising roof. Note on the right (against the wardrobe side) is the original, orange-coloured, Perspex tray; this period Dormobile accessory is so often missing from remaining examples and very difficult to obtain.

TOP RIGHT: A rather nice period accessory is this Easicool storage cabinet, which was an optional extra, and, despite the crude nature of its basic design, they did, and, in fact, do still work.

MIDDLE RIGHT: In the opposite corner to the Easicool cabinet is the plastic freshwater container. The blue (modern) hose leading from the top of the container delivers water to the sink by the hand pump; there is also a brass tap at the base.

BOTTOM RIGHT: The space within the rear doors was not wasted by the Dormobile design team, and seen here is one of the storage flaps cut into the rear door cards. Through constant use and age, the hinge area on these flaps eventually begins to rip slightly, this example has fared better than many.

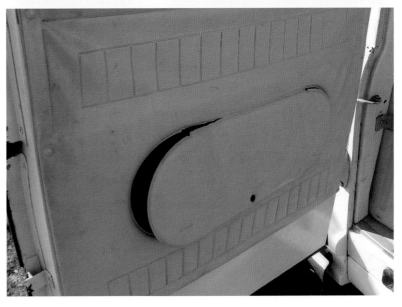

sides were long windows with sliding panels and a Dormobile 'air-scoop' window was placed near the cooker to aid the expulsion of cooking smells and condensation.

The forward dinette/seating area was centred on the famous Dormatic seats, which were capable of being turned in every way imaginable. Not only could they face forward and also reverse, it was also possible to fold them up completely against the vehicle sides in order to carry bulky items. At night these seats could be altered to form either two single beds or one double. Two stretcher bunks were housed in the cavernous rising roof. The floor covering in the Romany range differed with each model: linoleum, rubber and PVC coverings were used. The two gas cylinders were housed within special compartments in the vehicle floor; a metal container was also housed in the floor and this could be used either for further storage or as a chemical toilet.

The large, side-hinged Dormobile rising roof gave ample standing room within the vehicle; this was fitted with opening roof lights/ventilators. Curtains were fitted as standard to all windows and electric lighting was another standard fitment. Optional extras available for the Romany formed quite an exhaustive list as one would expect from Dormobile, but, as with most panel-van conversions of the period, the list did include a refrigerator. Prices for the Romany by 1967 had risen to £872 for the Super model and £947 for the De Luxe. Due to the large numbers produced over a significant period,

many examples have survived. It is worth pointing out that many of the several Dormobile models have by now undergone some degree of restoration and some owners have taken that opportunity to make minor changes, sometimes adding bits from another model within the range; as a result few surviving examples will now be in their original, factory condition.

LEFT: *This is the view from the rear, looking into the raised roof area, with one bunk in position for sleeping and the other still rolled up. The metal 'hoop' system can be seen here attached to the candy-stripe canvas and held with vinyl clips/loops.*

ABOVE: *Just about the most famous rising roof in the history of camper vans, the Dormobile pram-hood design. First fitted as a much smaller version in the mid 1950s, it evolved over the years with detailed minor improvements and modifications. The fibreglass roof capping was well built, though the roof vents on many models are often cracked requiring repair or complete replacement; spares are still available.*

LEFT: *A view of the Romany interior, basic and yet very functional. Martin Walter Ltd produced thousands of examples between 1957 through to the demise of the CA in 1969. They also produced an up-market version with a beautiful wooden interior, the Deauville.*

4

Calthorpe Home-Cruiser
(Bedford CA)

Press picture of the Calthorpe Home-Cruiser, the Maurice Calthorpe conversion based on the Bedford CA with its distinctive arched rising roof outline. This panel-van conversion on the CA van was released in 1958 to replace the earlier (1957) Calthorpe coach-built example, also on the CA. The Calthorpe-designed rising roof was the first such to be fitted to production camper vans in Britain, and was also available to other converters.

I have already mentioned the first post-Second World War production motor-caravan released by Maurice Calthorpe early in 1957; although that was a coach-built model, it still featured the Calthorpe rising roof, the first of its kind in Britain to be fitted to a motorcaravan. However, that first vehicle by Maurice Calthorpe is believed to have sold in very small numbers; it was quickly deleted by Calthorpe and replaced by a more conventional panel-van conversion, again on the Bedford CA but once more featuring the Calthorpe rising roof. This model proved to be far more popular with buyers and sold in greater numbers. It is this panel-van conversion that I feature here.

Maurice Calthorpe will, no doubt, best be remembered in motorcaravanning history as the man who designed

and patented the first British rising roof. In addition to this achievement, one should not overlook his excellent designs with regard to interiors. The Home-Cruiser range was well received from the outset in the 1950s; models were available on several chassis throughout production, including the Austin 152, the BMC J4, the Bedford CA, the Commer, the Ford Thames and the Standard Atlas. As the primary focus of this book is Bedford motorcaravans, I will concentrate on the Calthorpe CA vehicle for description purposes.

The Home-Cruiser conversion on the Bedford CA base vehicle had the familiar interior layout, so popular on panel-van conversions of the period. On entering the rear of the Bedford through the double doors there was a long, upholstered seat running the

length of the van on the right-hand side. This seat was certainly multi-functional – it could form a seating 'divan' for four people, a dinette (with table) again for four, and a single bed in the evening. When pulled down and out it was transformed into a full double bed. Along the left-hand side was the kitchen and wardrobe, as with the Ford Thames model, and the cabinet work was in light oak with mahogany trim. The kitchen contained a sink, two-burner cooker with grill and storage cupboards beneath. The wardrobe was situated next to the kitchen in the left-hand corner of the vehicle. A Home-Cruiser based on the Bedford was available on both the 10/12 or the 15cwt base vehicle, and one clever use of space on the Bedford was the alteration of the front bench seat in the cab.

Calthorpe Home-Cruiser (Bedford CA)

LEFT: *This is the front view of the only known surviving Calthorpe coach-built example, which was released in 1957, based on the early Bedford CA with 'split' windscreen and rudimentary grille. This survivor is still sporting its original paintwork.*

RIGHT: *Side view of the same vehicle, and, despite the fact that Maurice Calthorpe had produced a coach-built body on the CA chassis, he curiously chose to fit his rising roof rather than increase the headroom in the living area in the first place. This particular example is now in the safe hands of a Bedford enthusiast after it had stood in a lock-up garage outside London undisturbed for over thirty years.*

This bench seat could be reversed to face the interior living space, thus providing seating for six people when combined with the standard seat, which ran the length of the Bedford. This design feature was significant in motorcaravan history and development. Calthorpe and, earlier, Martin Walter Ltd (Dormobile) both installed this seating arrangement, which allowed the driving compartment to form part of the interior living space. Despite the advantages of this seating system, few converters followed the trend. The irony of this is that nearly all modern motorcaravans (panel van and coach-built models) feature cab seats, which swivel around to form part of the living space. The front bench seat in the Bedford could also be arranged to lie flat and provide another double bed, in addition to the rear one.

The floor covering in the Bedford was vinyl and curtains were supplied for all windows. Interior lighting was supplied from both 12V electrics and gas. Water to the kitchen sink was delivered via a hand pump, drawn from a water porter situated in the cupboard below. The Bedford, of course, had the patented Calthorpe rising roof fitted as standard. The cost of a Bedford Home-Cruiser in 1960 was around £820, depending on which base option was specified. The registered office for M. Calthorpe (Home-Cruiser) Ltd was Park Lane (later Oxford Street) in central London, but these certainly were not the factory addresses. The coachbuilders F. Stuart & Son Ltd built many Home-Cruiser models in Shepperton and Home-Cruiser Coachworks Ltd, of Walton-on-Thames, Surrey, built later models.

Today we are all well aware that a motorcaravan can have a variety of uses, but during the infancy of this leisure activity the designers, coachbuilders and, indeed, the advertisers were trying extremely hard to get these points across to potential buyers. This is how the Calthorpe Home-Cruiser sales brochure sang the praises of its product in the late 1950s:

These two artists' illustrations show the interior of the Mk.II Calthorpe Home-Cruiser introduced at the 1958 Earls Court Motor Show. The top picture is the view from the rear looking toward the front of the vehicle, and the bottom picture shows the interior view when looking from the front to the rear.

With a Calthorpe 'Home Cruiser' the world is yours – smart resorts, beautiful country, woodlands, mountain resorts

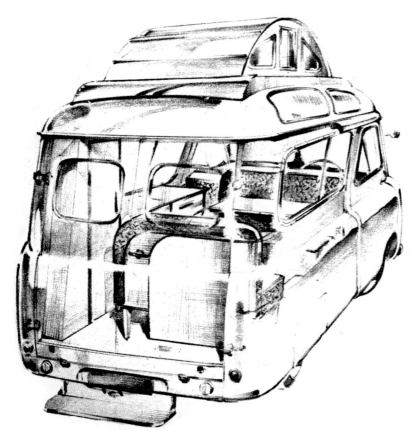

LEFT: Another artist's impression, but this time a cut-away illustration of the whole vehicle. The Home-Cruiser was produced from 1958 to the mid 1960s, though the few surviving examples lead one to assume that it was produced in quite limited numbers.

BELOW: This line drawing indicates the floor plan of the Home-Cruiser, with the dotted lines showing the bed set-up once the seats were extended at night. Some period literature does differ in so much detail that I have found the kitchen area pictured on the opposite side on occasions.

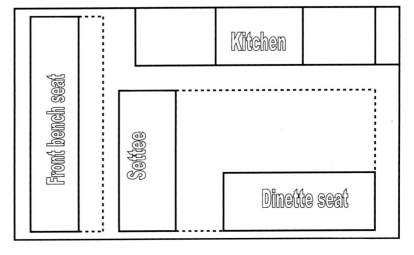

and gay cities – places which were only a distant hope are now attainable at a fraction of the cost, with none of the usual troubles of booking hotel accommodation, packing, unpacking, etc., and the inevitable bills and tipping. You simply hang your clothes in the wardrobe, place your travelling necessities in the spacious lockers and drive wherever you wish, completely independent and free of tiresome and often expensive accommodation arrangements.

At the outset I mentioned a coach-built example produced by Maurice Calthorpe in very limited numbers during 1957, so limited, in fact, that it was until very recently widely accepted that none had survived. An advertisement for a vintage Bedford motorhome appeared in a classic vehicle publication a couple of years ago and was seen by fellow motorcaravan historian John Hanson of Leeds, who duly contacted me to point it out. To my amazement I discovered that it was one of the early Calthorpe coach-built examples, and telephoned the seller to establish whether it was still for sale; it was, but only just. The seller was disposing of the Bedford for his uncle and pointed out that time was of the essence because the vehicle was in a lock-up garage on the outskirts of London and needed to be moved quickly. It seemed that the vehicle had been in the garage since 1972 and was completely intact. But to remove the vehicle would not be straightforward, I was told, as the garage door had dropped and the approach to it was thick with overgrown bramble. Sadly, negotiations with the seller broke down quite quickly and he was threatening to send it for scrap. Many months passed until one day I was approached by someone who told me that he had taken delivery of an early Bedford CA motorhome dating from 1957, making the point that it was a coach-built motorhome, not a camper van with a lifting roof. If it was a coach-built and it did date from 1957, then I assumed it could only be the Calthorpe model, so I asked the owner to send me some pictures by email for identification purposes. It turned out to be the very example that had been in the London garage since 1972, and the seller had indeed carried out his threat to send it for scrap. Thankfully, the person charged with removing the Bedford realized that it could be an important model, given the age and the unique bodywork, and

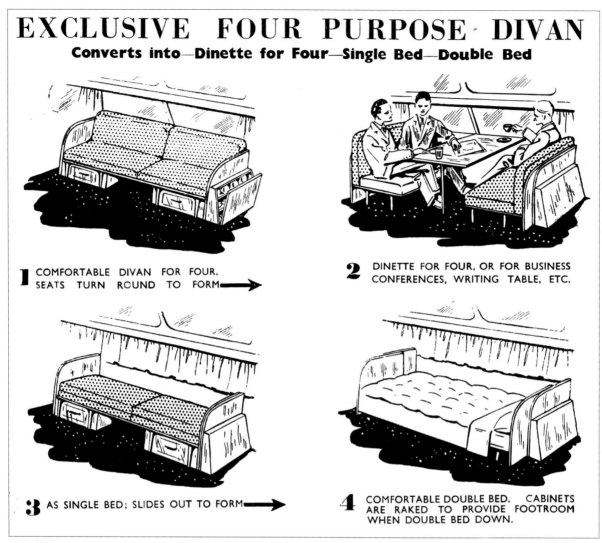

EXCLUSIVE FOUR PURPOSE · DIVAN
Converts into—Dinette for Four—Single Bed—Double Bed

1 COMFORTABLE DIVAN FOR FOUR. SEATS TURN ROUND TO FORM ➡

2 DINETTE FOR FOUR, OR FOR BUSINESS CONFERENCES, WRITING TABLE, ETC.

3 AS SINGLE BED; SLIDES OUT TO FORM ➡

4 COMFORTABLE DOUBLE BED. CABINETS ARE RAKED TO PROVIDE FOOTROOM WHEN DOUBLE BED DOWN.

These interesting diagrams are reproduced from a Calthorpe sales brochure dating from 1959 showing potential buyers the benefit of the four-person divan.

how right he was. That person was aware of Classic Vauxhall Services in Surrey and spoke to them; they also saw its potential and, I am pleased to say, that the only 'known' Calthorpe coach-built from that period is now back on the road and being displayed at classic vehicle shows in Britain, and, although it has yet to be given a full restoration, it is at least now roadworthy again. It is a story that could so easily have had a sad ending, but thanks to the diligence of one person an important part of British motorhome history is safe and well.

If the coach-built example of the early Calthorpe is regarded as something of a rarity, then the same must surely apply to the more popular Calthorpe rising-roof model, despite the fact that this model was produced in far greater numbers. During the early 1990s, when I first formed the Classic Camper Club, I was aware of at least three surviving

Calthorpes based on the Bedford CA chassis, but today I am aware of just a single example in the hands of a classic enthusiast. I am not for a moment suggesting that there is only one Bedford CA Calthorpe panel-van example in existence as it is highly likely that more have survived, perhaps kept in dry storage for restoration at a later date; at least it would be nice to think so. As for other chassis with a Calthorpe conversion, I'm pleased to say that a couple of Ford Thames models are still in use; so too is a Standard Atlas example and at least two based on the BMC J4 van. As an avid Commer enthusiast I am very pleased that at least two examples based on the Rootes light commercial are known to me, and these are safely in the hands of dedicated enthusiasts.

I'm sure that many people of a 'certain age' will remember the lovely old British Pathe newsreels that were

shown in cinemas around the UK for so many years, and it is thanks to them that a real gem of motorcaravan history has survived relating to the Calthorpe models. In June of 1957 British Pathe made a very short film (one minute eight seconds, and in colour) that featured the coach-built model, Maurice Calthorpe as the driver and no less than the celebrated actress Dora Bryan as his guest passenger, together with another female and one male occupant. This short film (with sound) can be viewed on the home computer and is well worth looking at, and there is even a scene featuring the female passenger taking a dip in the bath tub that was housed beneath the front bench seat! To view this piece of classic camper nostalgia simply log on to www.britishpathe.com and type the words 'Home on wheels 1957' into the search menu – enjoy!

TOP: One of the few remaining examples of the Calthorpe Home-Cruiser, once owned by Alan Kirtley of Bedfordshire: Alan rescued the vehicle from being crushed and carried out a full restoration, later picking up several awards at vehicle shows and rallies.

ABOVE: The same early 1960s Home-Cruiser, shown here with the roof down. Calthorpe produced the Home-Cruiser range of camper vans on a variety of chassis, which included the Bedford CA, Commer, Ford Thames and Standard Atlas.

RIGHT: Interior of the Calthorpe Home-Cruiser as seen from the rear. Bench seat in the cab area, kitchen and wardrobe to the left, the four-person divan/settee to the right and storage pockets in the rear door cavity.

5
Dormobile Debonair (Bedford CA)

ABOVE: *A number of Debonair examples have survived in the hands of dedicated enthusiasts, and the vehicle seen here is a prime candidate. Owned and maintained by Robin Phillips, it always had many admirers when in use for camping weekends and on display at classic vehicle events.*

LEFT: *The Dormobile Debonair was first unveiled at the 1964 Motor Show, a whole new concept in motorcaravan design as the vehicle was manufactured from fibreglass, apart from the Bedford CA frontal area. It proved to be an instant success and hundreds were produced at the Folkestone factory. This example was seen at a classic camper van rally.*

Released by Martin Walter Ltd in 1964, the Dormobile Debonair certainly took centre stage for innovative design and styling. In fact, the Debonair could not easily be classified – it was not a coach-built example in the traditional sense of aluminium sheets over a wooden frame, neither was it a panel-van conversion. The craftsmen at the Folkestone factory broke new ground by constructing a motorcaravan using a two-piece, fibre-glass-moulded model. Due to the long association the company had with Vauxhall Motors, the Debonair was available based only on the Bedford CA, 15/17cwt base. Only the small CA metal bonnet and grille section were retained, the remainder of the vehicle was a complete GRP moulding. The Debonair, released in 1964, continued in production on the Bedford CA until the introduction of the new Bedford CF in 1969. It was then restyled for the new base vehicle. For the purpose of this description I am concentrating on a model from 1966.

The Dormobile design team certainly brought all their years of experience to the fore when committing the Debonair to paper. This model had one of the most distinctive exteriors of any motorcaravan from the classic period. The front end was distinctively Bedford CA and just above the windscreen two separate, long windows were added for extra internal light. Two further deep quadrant windows were placed on either side of the windscreen, giving the driver excellent views of the road, yet at the same time allowing even more light into the interior. At the rear of the vehicle were more beautifully shaped windows, letting the light come flooding into the rear section. The GRP body afforded full standing height in the interior and two opening roof ventilators were fitted as standard. The interior of this model was neatly divided into two sections, or 'cabins' as Dormobile referred to them. The forward area contained the cooker, an Easicool food storage cabinet (or optional refrigerator) and forward-facing seats for five people. The rear cabin was fitted with lounge-type seating, which became the dinette when the table was erected.

On opening the one-piece rear door one first saw the lounge/dinette. With seating to each side of the vehicle, a table (stored beneath a seat and with a textile covering) could be erected with the aid of two metal legs and was placed between the seats for dining. The remainder of this 'cabin' consisted of eye-level storage lockers, with further storage beneath the seat bases. The dinette seats converted at night into a double bed. All exterior surfaces in the dinette/lounge were finished in a wood veneer. Two good-sized wardrobes were also in this area of the vehicle, situated near the middle on each side. When viewed from the rear, a tall cupboard could be seen on the left, next to a wardrobe, this housing the toilet, and there was a square louvred window mounted quite high within this cubicle. The forward 'cabin' was another seating area; this contained forward-facing seats for five (including the driver) and these seats converted into a second double bed. Easy access to the frontal area could be gained (in addition to that in the rear) via the passenger cab door. The kitchen in the Debonair was extremely well planned for such a confined space, with the possible exception of the refrigerator, as this was situated in a slightly awkward position opposite the cooker in a narrow

gap. The stainless steel sink was housed in the dividing cupboard, which separated the front and the rear areas. Water was pumped to the sink via a foot-operated system; this in turn came from three 3gal containers. The containers were accessed through a floor well, the floor section being clipped to a bracket on the seat (a water heater was an optional extra). Gas bottles were also housed in the floor, again a floor section was removable for access, and this was near the toilet/sink area. The cooker, with oven, was placed near the toilet and wardrobe, just behind the passenger seat. The cooker had a fold-up worktop and there was high mounted storage cupboard above. Surfaces in the forward area were finished in a bright, hardwearing laminate. The Easicool storage cabinet (or optional refrigerator) was beneath the sink and accessed from the end.

At this point I must mention the clever folding door/flap system employed by Dormobile on this model. The designers certainly had not missed a trick on the Debonair and even came up with a

simple way of dividing the front and the rear cabins by means of both the toilet door and other flaps. These were bolted into fittings to provide the Debonair interior with two completely separate areas, ideal for privacy.

During my research I found a recurring theme when reading about previous test reports of this model carried out over the years since its introduction. Everyone mentioned the enormous amount of storage space that Dormobile had managed to fit into this unique motorcaravan, given its dimensions. It was clearly designed by someone who had actually used a motorcaravan, which, surprisingly, was not always the case with some conversions.

Curtains were fitted as standard to all windows on this model and fluorescent lighting was fitted to both the rear and the forward areas. Martin Walter Ltd offered a bewildering array of options for all Dormobile models, and the Debonair was no exception. Basic options for the Bedford CA base vehicle were a four-speed gearbox (in place of the standard three-speed); a diesel

RIGHT: This was an excellent marketing tool back in 1964, not only did Martin Walter Ltd publicize their new model in the general motoring press, but they used a clever cut-away diagram in order to reveal the interior layout and fitments – it obviously worked.

engine was an extra £125 in late 1966 and early 1967. Specific to this model was the option of a refrigerator in place of the Easicool cabinet at £45, a water heater at £35 and concertina-style blinds for the windows above the cab at £3.5s. The price listing for a Dormobile Debonair early in 1967 was £1,298 in the basic/standard form. One interesting feature to note in relation to this model concerned the exterior colour; paint colours on the Debonair GRP body were bonded into the shell during manufacture, a unique feature for this period. The standard Dormobile colours for the main body area were (in 1967) Dormobile White, Iris Blue, Foam Grey and Lime Green. The nose section, top coach line and vehicle side flash could be painted in any Martin Walter colour, of which there were many. As a point of reference, by far the most common colour combination for the Debonair was to have the main body in Dormobile White with the coach lines in a burgundy/red. The sales brochure of the period stated that 'repainting could be forgotten – the colour, bonded into the material during manufacture, keeps its lustre'. I do not believe that Martin Walter thought for a moment that Debonair models would still be in use forty years later! Colour fading has now occurred on many surviving examples due to weathering, and repainting has had to be undertaken.

The Bedford CA Dormobile Debonair was a great success story for the

Robin Phillips' example again, offering a closer view of the front section and the additional windows above the windscreen.

Folkestone company; it was hugely popular from the outset in 1964, received excellent press reviews and, indeed, remains a much sought-after classic motorcaravan even today.

CF DEBONAIR

When production of the Bedford CA finally ceased, to be replaced by the CF model in 1969, the Debonair name was carried over to the new model in the form of the Dormobile Debonair II.

If you are building a top-selling camper van and the base vehicle is

withdrawn by the manufacturer, what do you do? In the case of Dormobile you simply switch that winning design over to another vehicle, and such was the case with the Debonair bodywork. The ground-breaking GRP body design of the Debonair was first seen in 1964 on the hugely popular Bedford CA chassis. The marriage between the Bedford and the Debonair design was a big hit with British buyers – here at last was a motorcaravan body that would not leak with age (due to the lack of joints), was light and had a spacious, well designed interior. It was also mated to one of the most popular base vehicles of the period and, as a result, it sold in significant numbers. But in 1969 Vauxhall decided to drop the ageing CA model (in production since 1952) in favour of the CF model.

What happened next was quite remarkable as Vauxhall had given Dormobile some of the new CF chassis very early in production, the result being that Dormobile unveiled the new Debonair (and the Romany) on the CF chassis before the 'new' CF range of light vans was officially launched. Although the new CF was different in every way from the earlier CA, there was little by way of change with regard to the Debonair, which was hardly surprising given the earlier model's popularity.

The Mk.II Debonair was based on the Bedford CF 106in wheelbase chassis and was initially powered by the 1599cc petrol engine. Here is the Dormobile

Driver's side front view of the fibreglass Debonair body, showing the sliding door-window glass and the flowing external lines of the front wing. The coloured bands on the body were impregnated during construction and not painted on later in the traditional style.

description from one of the first Mk.II Debonair sales brochures:

The new Bedford Dormobile Debonair Mk.II is the ultimate in caravan luxury. Join the motor-caravanning elite in the new Dormobile Debonair Mk.II – built for discerning families big or small, by craftsmen from Dormobile, the people who began it all. It is interesting to note that some big hire fleets make extensive use of Debonairs, a sure sign of its practicality and roadworthiness. There is a choice of eleven attractive Dormobile colours for the body side flash. All resin-bonded moulding is in Dormobile white.

The Debonair Mk.I was the motor caravan perfectionist's dream. The new Debonair Mk.II is still that, and now the ultimate in luxury. The Debonair Mk.II is built to give years of reliable performance and caravanning pleasure. The new Debonair is exclusively for seekers after comfort – yet it seats as many as eight people in luxury! And what luxury – all upholstery is in a quilted nylon mixture fabric and stitched in nylon for sure! The body is constructed of colour-impregnated, reinforced moulded glass fibre, proof against corrosion, and its own garage all year through!

I shall not dwell in great detail on this particular Dormobile model since to a certain extent I would simply be reiterating what has already been written about the Mk.I Debonair. The Mk.II version was almost a carbon-copy of that first example, give or take a few dimensions and minor modifications. Suffice it to say the Mk.II model was a very well equipped camper van for the period (1969). A major feature of the Debonair in both the Mk.I and the Mk.II format was the way in which the designers had split the internal space into two, ideal for a family with a couple of small children since they could be put to bed in one half while the parents stayed up later in the other; it was without doubt very well planned.

The Debonair Mk.II had seating for up to eight; the rear used the two bench-style seats, which also acted as the dining area, with the addition of a table. The front of the vehicle had two single seats in the driving cab and a double bench seat immediately behind, the front and the back of the interior were divided by the centrally located kitchen

The body of the Debonair contained a large amount of glass, especially at the front of the vehicle, which in turn afforded a good view for the driver. Seen here is the long, curved section to the side of the front windscreen, duplicated on the other side.

The rear section of the Debonair also contained large glazed areas, but this time in order to give occupants a good view of the scenery when stationary and sitting at the rear dinette. The backrest of the bench-style seat can just be seen through the window.

Dormobile Debonair (Bedford CA)

unit containing cupboards and the sink. Other internal fitments included a toilet cubicle housing a chemical toilet, a full cooker with oven alongside it and a full-length wardrobe on the opposite side. A refrigerator or Easicool cabinet was available as an option.

Other standard features of the Mk.II Debonair included curtains to all windows, water containers, fluorescent lighting, vanity mirror, opening caravan windows and a rear step to aid entrance through the one-piece door.

The CF Debonair was produced alongside the Bedford CF Land Cruiser (similar body, different interior) for a while, and late in 1971 a 4/5 berth Debonair cost around £1,994.

ABOVE: A much better view of the high front window sections just above the windscreen, which gave the driver and passenger excellent views when touring.

RIGHT: The Bedford CA Debonair is certainly a true classic motorhome with a loyal band of followers. This beautiful example formed the centrepiece of a classic motorcaravan display at a large motorhome show in Peterborough, gaining many admirers.

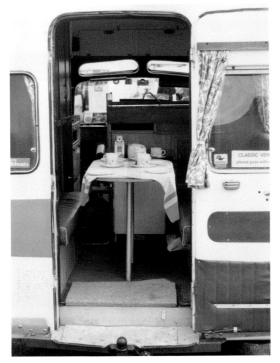

LEFT: The same Debonair on display, but this time as seen from the rear. The table is nicely arranged for afternoon tea and some internal fitments are clearly visible, such as the rear bench seats (also a double bed), centrally positioned sink/worktop, cooker on the far left and storage cupboards/toilet alongside.

BELOW: In 1969 the Bedford CA was replaced by the CF range and Martin Walter Ltd redesigned the Debonair body to fit the new CF chassis. The result was the Debonair Mk.II as seen here, and unveiled before the official release of the new CF.

obscure **Bedford CA** *camper vans*

Produced in the north-east of England, the Hadrian range of coach-built motorhomes were in production for the first half of the 1960s. The factory workforce are seen here proudly standing beside one of their creations.

Despite the popularity of the Bedford CA light van during the 1950s and the 1960s, few converters actually used it as a base for motorcaravan conversions. The huge success of the Martin Walter Dormobile Caravan has left many people with an enduring image of what the iconic 1950s–60s camping vehicle looked like. The Dormobile Caravan and the Calthorpe Home-Cruiser may, indeed, have had the lion's share of the Bedford CA camper-van market, but other, smaller converters did use the CA van in limited numbers. One should also remember that these two decades were a time of development and evolution for the British motorcaravan industry, which was then still very much in its infancy. As a result, many families who could not afford a fully fitted camper van turned their attention to fitting out their own light commercial vans, and the Bedford CA was a popular choice with many for this purpose.

If Martin Walter Ltd and Maurice Calthorpe were producing the bulk of the 'factory' conversions on the Bedford CA, who else was offering camper van models on the CA? A scan through the motorcaravan buyers' guides of the time would reveal the answer – very few. Most converters during the latter part of the 1950s were using the BMC J2 and the Ford Thames van, though the number of British camper-van converters at this time was small. At the start of the 1960s that number began to grow and one of the first 'production' coach-built motorhomes was then offered, based on the Bedford CA, this being the Hadrian by Motor Caravan Bodies Ltd in the north-east of England.

HADRIAN-BEDFORD CA

Motor Caravan Bodies Ltd, of Newburn, Newcastle-upon-Tyne, built the Hadrian range of coach-built motorcaravans; they were a coach-building company who were, at one time, specialist boat builders, later progressing into the increasingly popular motorcaravan industry. The name chosen for the range

of models to be offered was taken from the famous Roman wall in the north of Britain. The company produced motorcaravans for only around four to five years, but they do hold one claim to fame in the history and development of leisure vehicles, being the first company to offer a coach-built model for sale on the new release from Rootes in 1960, the Commer.

The Hadrian range included four models: they were the Ambassador on the Ford Thames 15cwt chassis, the Austral based on the Austin 152, the Bedouin on the Bedford CA and finally the Commanche on the Commer 15cwt. Judging by press articles and other publications, it appears that the most popular model was that based on the Commer, the Hadrian Commanche. But I should point out that the interior of each was pretty much a standard design. Consequently, in describing the Hadrian based on the Bedford CA, the reader can assume (apart from minor detail changes) that the Hadrian on the Rootes Commer, the BMC J2 and the Ford Thames all had

obscure Bedford CA camper vans

The Hadrian was available on several chassis, and, although a couple of Commer and Ford Thames examples have survived, I know of no remaining examples on the CA base. (Apologies for the poor quality of this period picture showing the rear and side of the Bedford Hadrian Bedouin model.)

BELOW: The Hadrian models were quality, hand-crafted motorhomes with a side-entrance door, mid-section dining area and rear kitchen. In this picture the kitchen facilities can be clearly seen located at the rear, with a full cooker/hob/oven, sink alongside and the optional refrigerator underneath. If the refrigerator was not specified, then this space became a storage cupboard.

The number of Hadrian examples still in use does not even run into double figures, and yet surviving examples do turn up from time to time, as this picture testifies. A Hadrian stored for many years in a barn on a British farm, it was, of course, snapped up by a classic vehicle enthusiast, but requires complete restoration because of water ingress.

similar layouts. The son of one of the original company owners revealed that the design for the Hadrian was, in fact, based on a trailer caravan that the family had used to tour Ireland. They certainly did manage to capture the caravan feel with the Hadrian design; even the external appearance owed much to the early touring caravans.

The Hadrian was rather box-like in appearance with a contoured roof constructed from three sections made from GRP. The rear section was perhaps the most elaborate design feature of the exterior, with a curved waistline and appealing aluminium beading to emphasize the detailing. The rear windows were in three sections, one-piece windows at each end with a square louvred window in the centre. The access flap for the water tank was also on the rear end. Entry to the living area was via a side-entrance door positioned just behind the passenger cab door. A fold-down step nicely recessed into the bottom of the door aided access to the vehicle. The top half of the entrance door was glazed and, again, the designer had used aluminium beading on the exterior of the door, which continued in a coach line/flash along the side of the Hadrian, just below the window line.

The kitchen facilities were located along the rear of the vehicle and included a sink, a cooker with oven and spacious storage units. Water was delivered to the sink by a hand pump located to one side of the sink. A cool cabinet was fitted as standard, although a refrigerator could be ordered as an option. In the nearside rear corner was an extremely large wardrobe, so big, in fact, that this was often used as a toilet compartment.

Eye-level storage lockers were in abundance all around the interior, and the space above the driving cab was more than large enough for all bedding and pillows. The table in the Hadrian was of the free-standing variety and dining took place in a central area of the vehicle. The Hadrian had four forward-facing seats (including those in the driving cab) and a longer bench-style seat toward the rear, near the kitchen. This seat converted into a double bed, as did the seats in the central part of the vehicle, making this a four-berth model. If a two-berth model were specified then the single seat directly behind the driver's seat was replaced by a narrow wardrobe.

The interior of the Hadrian was panelled in a light oak veneer; cupboard and door edges were also made from oak, with oak veneer again being used for the door inserts on cupboards. Fresh water was carried in a 10gal underfloor tank; a waste tank was also fitted to the vehicle's underside. All seating was covered with a textile upholstery fabric in several colour options. The standard floor covering was vinyl, but a carpet was available as an option and curtains were fitted to all windows as standard. Lighting within the living area was supplied from both gas and electric fitments.

The Hadrian motorhomes were certainly well constructed with a good interior design. But despite the fact that they were available for about five years, few examples have survived, and none to my knowledge on the Bedford CA. Although I have described the Bedford CA Bedouin four-berth model, I list the price of all the models in the 1964 line-up:

- Hadrian Ambassador (Ford Thames), £1,060
- Hadrian Austral (Austin 152), £1,090
- Hadrian Bedouin (Bedford CA), £1,083
- Hadrian Commanche (on the Commer), £1,083.

BEDFORD CA PEGASUS

The first news of this particular conversion appeared in the motorcaravan press during the early 1960s as the Mk.II Pegasus, a conversion on the LWB CA chassis featuring a rising roof operated by compressed air.

Despite repeated efforts, I have been unable to find any mention of a Mk.I

Not a model I have ever seen in the flesh, though, of course, there could be a survivor sitting in a barn or lock-up somewhere, this is the Pegasus, based on the LWB Bedford CA chassis and dating from about 1965. Fibreglass panels have been used to create an extended body with side-entry door, with rising roof in the lowered position. The model seen here is the Mk.II version; at the time (1965), Pegasus Tourers were based in Lancashire.

The Mk.IIIA model Pegasus, this time from 1966 and by then featuring a fibreglass high top as opposed to the earlier rising roof.

A rare period advertisement for the Pegasus model, this dates from 1966 and publicizes the Mk.IIIA option; note that the company by this time were based in Glasgow.

Pegasus, but one cannot asssume that it did not exist, perhaps only a very small number were built or it could be that Mk.I was merely the prototype. Either way, the Pegasus model in the Mk.II and the Mk.III variant marked a rather short-lived venture, as the literature of the time carried advertisements for the models for only around four years.

KENEX CAREFREE-BEDFORD CA

Kenex Coachwork Ltd of Dover were well-established coachbuilders when they entered into motorcaravan conversions in the late 1950s. They had built an array of special bodies for such vehicles as mobile shops and fire tenders, and, like so many established coachworks

then, they saw an opening for a new market when the leisure industry was expanding. The height of their success with regard to motorcaravan conversion came in the period 1960–3. Around this time they were taken over by Martin Walter in Folkestone, and the Kenex conversions disappeared from the listings. Conversions by Kenex were

ABOVE: *A period press-release photograph of the beautiful Bedford CA Kenex Carefree model of the early 1960s, with a Standard Atlas Kenex camper van just visible in the background. Kenex Coachworks were based in Dover and produced many utility vehicles in addition to camper vans, notably the Kene-Coach minibus. The motorcaravan side of the Kenex business was purchased by Martin Walter Ltd (Dormobile) around 1963.*

A period sales brochure cover for the Kenex Carefree model, and it is fair to say that this was the second-best-selling Bedford CA camper van of the period, but, even so, sales figures were not in the same league as those for the Bedford Dormobile.

ABOVE: The Kenex was fitted with a 'straight-up' style of rising roof operated from the interior by hinged poles. I have seen two styles of this roof fitted to Kenex models, one version that covered the entire roof section of the vehicle, and another that ended just short of the front roof section.

given the title Kenex Carefree, and models were available on the Bedford CA, the BMC J4, the Ford Thames (10/12/15 cwt) and the Standard Atlas.

Even before the Kenex company was absorbed into Martin Walter, the interior of a Kenex Carefree bore many similarities to that of a Dormobile motorcaravan. The layout, furniture styling and lay-flat beds all had traits of the Dormobile, although the rising roof on the Kenex was entirely different. Viewing the interior from the twin rear doors one found the kitchen unit to the left-hand side. This comprised a two-burner hob with grill and a sink with drainer. The entire area beneath the sink and the cooker was reserved solely for storage with twin sliding doors fitted, there was also a cutlery draw situated below the drainer. Lift-off worktops were fitted on top of the cooker and the sink, as opposed to the usual hinged variety found in most models. A combined pump/tap was placed

Another period sales picture, this time illustrating the Kenex interior, which was not unlike that of the Bedford Dormobile in terms of design and style.

beside the sink and water was delivered there from a 7gal tank housed under the vehicle floor. On the opposite side to the kitchen was a full-height wardrobe, with a hinged mirror attached to the front of it. Next to the wardrobe was another, much smaller cupboard

fitted with a drawer and a door below. On the side of the wardrobe was a gaslight, and there was an additional electric light in the vehicle. A combined seat/step had been incorporated with the base of the wardrobe, primarily for use as a seat when cooking; this pulled

Apologies for the poor quality of this picture, but photographs of the early Bedmobile model by Taylor Motor Bodies are as rare as the real thing. Needless to say, there are no known surviving examples of this model from the early 1960s with its strange, roof-mounted, double bed.

out when required and neatly stowed away when not in use.

Four single seats were fitted in the Kenex interior, including the two cab seats. All were were covered with PVC and finished with piping around the edges. All four were forward facing for travelling. When it came to making up the beds, all the seats were required since they all lay flat, the seats on either side then butted together to form two single beds (the restricted width of the Ford Thames did not allow for transverse beds). Two full-length, single-stretcher bunks were housed in the rising roof; these rolled up neatly when not in use. For dining a laminate-topped table clipped to the interior wall of the vehicle, although to seat four around it, due to the seating position, was not the easiest of tasks.

ABOVE: Another picture of dubious quality, this time of another Bedmobile version fitted with a more traditional design of rising roof.

LEFT: Bennett & Patching of Worthing, Sussex produced this prototype model on the Bedford CA during the late 1950s. I have no record of its being put into full time production, and do not recall any road tests or advertisements appearing in the motoring press. The company later produced the sought-after Mini Wildgoose camper van.

A mystery Bedford CA motorhome dating from the 1950s: a coach-built example with a rear, side-entrance door and possibly constructed from aluminium panels.

Hidden within the floor of the Kenex were three trap-door panels, one for the water filler, one for the gas bottle storage and one for the battery; the floor covering was of the vinyl type. All cabinet/cupboards in the interior were finished in a hard-wearing, patterned laminate with wooden edging. The Kenex interior was light and airy due to the standard fitment of windows to all sides and the rear doors. The Ford Thames also had a side-opening door, glazed on the top half. Curtains were fitted to all windows as standard. Optional extras on this model included a vehicle heater, chrome bumpers, padded engine cover (the engine was in the cab on the Ford Thames), fog lights and a radio. A fire extinguisher was standard and this was situated on the side of the wardrobe near the rear doors.

One notable feature of the Kenex Carefree models, which gained excellent revues in road tests, was the full-width, rising roof. It was of the type that lifted straight up by means of a metal framework, springs and pivots. It featured a GRP roof capping, which had a large amber ventilator fitted within it. The side and end panels were constructed from a strong, flexible fabric and coloured with contrasting horizontal stripes.

Using the year 1961 as a guide for prices, the Ford Thames Kenex Carefree carried a price tag of £813. Other models were priced as follows: the Bedford CA £785, the BMC J4 £805 and the Standard Atlas £810. The Kenex Carefree was good value for money as a panel-van conversion then, and, as a comparison, the following cars of the time were priced thus:

- Austin A55 Countryman, £914
- Ford Consul De Luxe, £823
- Ford Zodiac, £957
- Morris Traveller, £669.

Today there is a far greater difference in price between panel-van conversion motorcaravans and the average family saloon car.

7 Dormobile Roma (Bedford HA)

The Bedford HA Roma by Dormobile, 'small enough to fit in your garage' was the sales slogan during the 1960s. The Roma falls into the micro-camper category, being more of a picnic or occasional camper van, though there were and still are some owners who attach an awning to the vehicle and set off touring. The lovely example seen here is owned by Sean Browes of County Armagh, who is in the process of restoring it to its former glory.

The Roma based on the Bedford HA van was certainly one of the smallest camper vans offered by Dormobile, and, alongside their Ford Escort Elba, these were a pair of micro-campers in the Dormobile range. The diminutive Dormobile Roma was first unveiled at the 1967 Motor Show and caused quite a stir as this was the first car-derived camper to be offered by the Folkestone company. Based on the Bedford HA 8cwt van, and fitted with the 1159cc Vauxhall engine, the Roma was advertised as the camper van that would easily fit into the average garage. The design staff at Martin Walter Ltd did do an excellent job of squeezing a quart into a pint pot, with the Roma having all the interior fittings of much larger models, but in miniature. In one publication of the time I discovered an interview with a member of the sales team at Martin Walter relating to the introduction of the Dormobile Roma. He

stated that the number one target for sales of the Roma were, in fact, established motorcaravanners who already had a larger model and might then purchase the little Roma as their everyday car. But, as it happened, the Roma actually established a whole new market and introduced many newcomers to the joys of motorcaravanning.

'Drive small–park tall' was the slogan used to sell the Roma, and it certainly worked as sales within the first year exceeded expectations. This is how Martin Walter set about selling the Dormobile Roma in the motoring press:

Our little Roma has given berths to a family of three – our little Roma stands 5ft 6ins on her wheels. She measures only 12½ft long by 5ft wide yet she can sleep you, your wife and child.

With the roof raised and back extended, there's an extra 9½sq ft of floor space. Then you can unfold a 6ft double

bed out of the back seats. And pull down a 5ft 10ins bunk from the roof. (All your bedding, clothes and luggage will go in the three storage compartments.)

Just so your family never wants for a wash or a hot snack, there's even a fold-away cooker and sink unit. For all her family ways, the Roma is still a lively, little Bedford 8cwt at heart. At the end of the day, she fits snugly in a 14ft garage!

The most distinguishing feature of the Roma was, of course, the rising roof, a scaled-down version of the same side-hinged design found on so many Dormobile camper vans. The roof was fitted over the whole of the Bedford roof area. As one might expect, Dormatic seating formed the basis of the cleverly designed interior, with the two front Bedford seats being retrimmed with material to match the folding rear double-bench seat. An addition to the standard front seats was an occasional

ABOVE: Front view of the Roma with doors open and the roof in the raised position; note the Dormobile side flash in contrasting colour.

RIGHT: This is the earlier version of the Dormobile Roma with the solid-sided rear extension and top-hinged rear door/tailgate; the later variation had a rear canopy and a bottom-hinged door/tailgate.

BELOW LEFT: A nice close-up shot of the famous Dormobile rising roof, though this version is considerably smaller than that found on the Bedford CA and others. Despite its smaller size, it operates by exactly the same principle as the bigger variant, though this roof capping has only one roof vent and one window.

BELOW RIGHT: A rear/side angle shot of the Roma.

Dormobile Roma (Bedford HA)

The Roma was based on the basic Bedford HA light delivery van, so when it came to the cab layout it was strictly a no-frills affair, but this one has had some modification.

Everything in the Roma interior is in miniature, including the sink and cooker. In this picture the owner Sean Browes is seen operating the tiny gas cooker, which consists of top burners and a grill and has been swung out from its travelling position. The plastic sink is also visible here in its storage position, tipped up against the interior.

Not quite tucked up in bed all snug, but here Sean has laid out the rear bench seat in order to demonstrate the double set-up, which does, of course, utilize the rear extension canopy.

folding stool, which was attached to the back of the passenger seat; this was intended as a seat to aid the person using the small cooker. The rear bench seat was built on a tubular steel frame and a lever was pulled to enable the seat to lie flat in order to form the double bed. But in order to do this the design team had decided to make the rear an extension of the interior by means of an enclosed section utilizing the vehicle tailgate. With the one-piece, rear tailgate lifted up, two folding fibreglass panels then swing out to make the side walls of the rear extension. Double folding wooden panels then formed the extended floor, with a further wooden section (fitted with a cushion) taken from behind the rear seat and stood on its folding legs in order to make the rear section of the double bed. As if this procedure were not complicated enough, another fibreglass panel has then to be removed from its cradle in the van roof and fitted to the side and end panels to form the completed extension. This extension gave an extra internal area measuring 3ft × 3ft. It will not surprise you to learn that Martin Walter Ltd decided to dispense with this design from 1969 and launched a Mk.II version of the Roma, which had a mini pram-type hood fitted as the rear extension, with material matching that of the rising roof, an all together better design, and which, when in place, complimented the little Bedford far more than the cumbersome fibreglass design of the Mk.I.

The main rising roof on the Roma was obviously a scaled-down version of the full Dormobile roof, and, to this end, it contained only one stretcher bunk, measuring 5ft 7in in length and 1ft 7in wide, for a child. The bunk was rolled up when not in use and stored (via clips) against the rising roof aperture. With the lower and the upper bunk in place, it obviously required quite a strict routine to be put in place to use the limited amount of floor space.

Cooking in the Roma was by means of a very small Tilley, a single-plate hob and grill, which would swivel out from the side of the vehicle and lock into place for use; this was positioned immediately behind the driver's seat. Beside the cooker was the small tip-up-style sink, which, when raised would drain the contents through a built-in hose, routed through the floor of the

Roma. Beneath the hob and the sink was a storage cupboard with a single hinged door, and above the kitchen was a useful shelf (level with the rising roof aperture). Water was carried in two 3gal plastic containers, one of which was housed under the dashboard (passenger side) and the other behind the driver's seat. A small water pump was fitted to the Mk.II Roma, after complaints about the cumbersome job of lifting these water containers.

As one might imagine, storage space in the Roma was not vast. Apart from the kitchen cupboard already mentioned, there was a wardrobe to the nearside rear giving hanging space for a limited amount of clothing. Additional space was located in two cupboards, just below roof level and to the rear (on either side of the rear bench seat). Two storage pockets were also built into the rear door. As the rising roof covered the entire top of the Bedford, there was no room for a roof rack, with the result that any exterior annex/awning had to be carried in the vehicle when travelling. Curtains were supplied as standard to all windows and lighting was by a single electric unit positioned above the kitchen area. The single gas cylinder used for cooking was stored in a recess in the rear, behind the bench seat. For dining, two very small tables were supplied, which clipped into a recess on either side of the rear bench seat.

Naturally, a huge number of optional extras were available for the Roma owner, one of which was an extension tent giving valuable extra room when touring. A full list of camping accessories was available from the Martin Walter catalogue. The price of a Dormobile Roma Mk.II in the summer of 1969 was £825 for the three-berth De Luxe, and £795 for the two-berth model.

Despite quite a large number of Roma models being produced between 1967 and the mid 1970s, it would appear that few good examples have survived the passage of time. There are certainly no more than a dozen in regular use in Britain. The Roma model was the last Dormobile camper to be fashioned by the famous Martin Walter designer Cecil Carte, who had been with the company since 1922; it was his design team that invented the brilliant Dormobile rising roof in the mid 1950s.

The rear seat in travelling mode, but in this instance the vehicle is stationary as Sean enjoys a good read. To the right of the picture is one of the small dining tables in use.

Sean has obviously decided to wash his hands as he is seen here lifting the sink into position; note also the aluminium cooker tucked away in its storage location. The curtains in the roof are a later addition, but I would guess that those on the right are original Dormobile standard issue, they have worn well.

This is the view toward the front of the interior, as seen from the rear seat position.

Dormobile Roma (Bedford HA)

A closer view of the Roma with the roof in the raised position and the rear canopy extended. With the passenger door ajar, it is clear to see that the front seat tilts forward to allow passenger access to the rear seat. Sean (and his dog) are big classic vehicle fans.

GET LOST
in a real Dormobile (by the people who invented them)

Places you've never seen. Places you've never been. Now you and your family are going there in a Dormobile. It could be a weekend on impulse. It might be the year's big holiday. Whatever it is, you get the feeling that you want to pack up and go and there's the Dormobile waiting . . .

Spacious seating. Space to stand, eat, cook, wash and sleep – in comfortable full sized beds. Wardrobe space, cupboard space and there's the famous elevating roof (Dormobile patent) that provides unequalled headroom, more sleeping space.

It's nothing like camping, living in a Dormobile: much more luxurious. And independent. It's nothing like a hotel: more personal, more freedom, no hotel bills. Your own home on wheels. Home where the children can roam free. Open up some new frontiers

for *your* family – there's a Dormobile that's just right for you and yours.

Dormobile opens up new frontiers

Please send me the Dormobile brochure. I am interested in :
Bedford ☐ B.M.C. ☐ Ford ☐ Land-Rover ☐ Volkswagen ☐
(Please tick appropriate square)

Name

Address

To Dormobile Limited,
Folkestone, Kent.
A member of the Martin Walter Group

The sales and design team at Martin Walter had developed a knack over the years of getting more than one model out of one of their existing vehicles, and so it was with the HA Roma camper van. With the 8cwt HA van they immediately spotted a market for an all-purpose estate vehicle, which in effect was an HA Roma without the rising roof and interior fittings. They introduced the 'Beagle' estate car based on the Bedford HA van, fitting the distinctive Dormobile side windows as later fitted to the Roma camper van, and installed a rear seat in order to carry passengers. The little HA began life with a 1057cc petrol engine, which, by the end of production in 1973, had been up-rated to 1256cc. A period advertisement for the Beagle dating from 1965 carried the slogan, 'Estate car with the Martin Walter pedigree', and the clever use of a Beagle dog picture alongside; the cost of a Beagle estate in 1965 was £620. Dormobile designer Cecil Carte took the Beagle estate car one step further: realizing that there was a niche market for a compact 'weekend' camper van model, he and his team added a scaled-down Dormobile roof and basic interior fitments: the Roma was born and the age of 'micro' camper-van models had arrived.

LEFT: An interesting period advertisement for the Dormobile Roma, extolling the virtues of 'getting lost'.

introduction of the *Bedford CF*

The first CF van to receive the full motorcaravan conversion in 1969 was the Romany II by Dormobile, a rising-roof model that took its model name from the previous CA version. The new CF Romany and its sister release of the same time, the Debonair II, were announced ahead of the official CF range release, such were the close ties formed over many years between Vauxhall and Martin Walter Ltd/Dormobile.

A replacement for the Bedford CA range was announced by Vauxhall Motors in the autumn of 1969, this new range given the designation letters 'CF'. The new CF was initially available in five basic model types and a choice of four engines, these were the 14 and 18cwt models with the 1599cc OHC petrol engine, and the 22, 25 and 35cwt models with the 1975cc OHC petrol engine. A Perkins 1760cc diesel engine was an alternative option on the 14, 18 and 22cwt vans, with a Perkins 2524cc diesel available on the 25 and 35cwt models.

There was also quite an array of body options announced for the CF; these were a van with sliding cab doors and double rear doors, a van with hinged cab doors and double rear doors, a van with hinged cab doors, a side-opening door and rear double doors and a chassis-cab, and a chassis-cowl for specialist body builders. The chassis-cowl bases were the types used by converters such as Martin Walter for the Debonair II, Jennings for the Roadrangers and CI/Motorised for the Bedouin and the Autohome model. The first motorcaravan converter to utilize the CF range in 1969 was Martin Walter/Dormobile for the Romany II (14cwt van), Debonair II (18 and 22cwt chassis-cowl) and Deauville (de luxe chassis with side door). Because

LEFT: It is quite unbelievable what some converters were able to do with a basic Bedford CF van, given that this is what they were faced with at the beginning of the process.

of their strong ties with Martin Walter/ Dormobile, Vauxhall Motors had allowed the Folkestone company early access to the new CF range of vans in order that they could be the first to release new CF camper vans.

As already stated, the CF range was announced late in 1969 and, as a consequence, CA production was brought to a close, but new, unregistered CA camper vans would then still have been sitting in showrooms around the country. It was for this reason that quite a number of CA campers were not registered until 1969 as the remaining stock was sold off, and usually at a discounted price owing to the introduction of a new Bedford range.

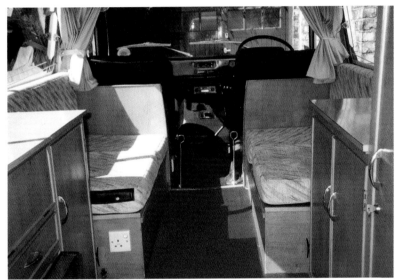

LEFT: This was the end result once Auto-Sleepers had applied their magic to the CF van interior, a camper van of the highest quality, craftsman-built in real wood.

BELOW: This rising roof Auto-Sleeper model proved very popular. It became a good seller throughout the 1970s and into the 1980s, and many fine examples are still in use today. Early 1970s sales success came to Dormobile in the shape of the CF Land Cruiser, in effect, a revised version of the Mk.II Debonair bodywork, but with a complete new interior.

Further Dormobile success came with the release of the Freeway model on the CF, which was also available on the Mk.I Ford Transit. An attractive overall appearance and good internal layout made the Freeway a firm favourite in the 1970s with buyers of rising-roof models.

An early coach-built example on the CF was the Bedouin model by CI/Autohomes of Poole, available in just one colour, and this is it – sandy/gold to reflect the model name.

The first full year of CF production (1970) saw the release of a new model from the giant CI company in Poole, Dorset; this was the Bedford Brigand, a traditional panel-van conversion fitted with the Parkestone rising roof. Dormobile also unveiled a new CF-based camper in 1970, the Contessa; a panel-van conversion fitted with the Dormobile roof, it had a simple interior with an untreated wood finish, allowing customers to varnish or paint it according to their own taste. The Contessa was deliberately kept under the significant £1,000 price figure in order to entice buyers. Both Dormobile and the newly introduced CF were enjoying great popularity in 1970 as the highly respected motorcaravan dealer Derek Turner placed an order for £30,000 worth of Dormobiles with the Folkestone-based converter.

New conversions on the Bedford CF were appearing thick and fast, and some were slightly more surprising than others. Searle had long been associated with their conversions on the go-anywhere Land Rover chassis for expedition use, the Carawagon, thus many were taken aback when the company unveiled a Carawagon conversion on the CF base, the Carawagon Express. In spring 1970 the established coach-builders J.H. Jennings, who had built a reputation for high quality with their Transit and Commer Roadranger motorhomes, released a Roadranger based on the CF. It was identical at first sight with all previous Roadranger models, except that the CF version had been fitted with a revised low-line roof, although the interior remained hand-crafted in real wood with the familiar rear entrance door. Two further coach-built models were released in 1970, these included the 'luxury' Bedford Debonair II, which was a revised, two-berth example fitted with the front seats from a Vauxhall Ventora car and carrying a price tag of £1,899. The other coach-built release of the year was the CI Bedouin, unveiled in a blaze of press publicity with a full Bedouin theme, including several tons of sand, palm trees, belly dancers and, of course, Bedouin tents. To add some degree of authenticity to the new model, this CI Bedouin was available in only one colour, a dark shade of gold, said to resemble desert sand. The buyers of the time were obviously impressed as the

Bedouin became an instant success and CI/M had yet another top-selling model in their expanding range.

By 1971 the CF had really established itself within the motorcaravan market and a plethora of new models began to appear. Auto-Sleepers, which had built a reputation for fine, hand-crafted interiors, first on the BMC J2 and then for the remainder of the 1960s on the Rootes/Chrysler Commer, unveiled a new addition to their model line-up, the Bedford CF Auto-Sleeper. A panel-van conversion with the superb rising roof, the interior was almost a carbon copy of that found in the Commer model, and it too became an instant hit with buyers, selling in huge numbers throughout the decade. Thankfully, a large number of these have survived and they do make an ideal first-time buy for those contemplating entering the world of classic camper vans. Another new model for 1971 came from Dormobile – the Freeway was a much modified version of the Romany II on the CF. This was a panel-van conversion fitted with the famous side-hinged roof, and featuring a GRP front roof luggage rack, neatly styled in order to compliment the GRP capping of the rising roof. The Freeway quickly became Dormobile's best selling model, and, in order to appeal to a greater proportion of the buyers, Dormobile also made the Freeway available on the Mk.I Ford Transit base. In its standard form (two-berth) the CF Freeway was priced at £1,489 on its release in September 1971, though a multitude of optional extras were available from the Dormobile leisure catalogue. The other notable release that year (in panel-van format) was the Richard Holdsworth CF conversion. Richard had begun converting vans during the late 1960s, mostly Volkswagens, and then added the Commer to his list. The Bedford CF was therefore a natural progression, given that it was by this time firmly established as a base vehicle with buyers. There were two more noteworthy additions to the motorcaravan buyers' guides before the end of 1971: Dormobile gave the Debonair II model a complete makeover and released the GRP-bodied Land Cruiser; and CI/M released a whole new concept in motorhome design, the Autohome. The CI Autohome was to be the first motorhome (in Britain) to be completely assembled independently

of the base vehicle. Designed by Carl Olsen, it was built on a wheeled jig within the factory, and then, once completed, was hoisted on to the rear chassis of the parent vehicle. The Autohome was initially released on the Mk.I Transit, but the option of the Bedford CF base quickly followed. Though no production records remain, it cannot be emphasized enough just what a huge success the Autohome was to become during the 1970s, not only on the Transit and the CF, but also on the Commer. With the on-going modifications, the CI Autohome became the CI Motorhome, again on the three familiar base vehicles.

A little over two years into CF production, Vauxhall Motors announced that there would be some improvements made to the CF range, most notably in the engine. In the spring of 1972 they decided to replace the 1599cc petrol unit with a larger capacity 1759cc engine (commonly referred to as the 1800cc). The 1975cc engine was replaced by the legendary 2279cc (2.3ltr) unit, which would become a firm favourite with Bedford/Vauxhall enthusiasts. Other changes at this time included the fitting of larger clutches, revised gear ratios and a new vehicle heater. Of course, 1972, when these engine improvements were made, would prove to be a significant milestone in British motorcaravan production history since this was the final year of sales before the introduction of VAT (value added tax). Converters were estimating that the magical sales figure of 20,000 motorcaravans would be sold in 1973, and some parts of the British motoring press put the figure even higher. It is still not clear today whether these figures were achieved, but they must have been very close; but what is certain, however, is that the introduction of VAT did have a marked impact on British sales of camper vans, which became apparent from around 1975 when the figures were published. Sales figures did tend to get distorted within the national industry, as the PR departments of the chassis suppliers, and the converters themselves laid claim to selling the greatest number of units. But despite this confusion, there is no doubt about the best selling base vehicles of the early 1970s, and in no particular order, these were: the Bedford CF, the Commer, the Ford Transit and the Volkswagen.

BEDFORD CF PRODUCTION

The following sequence of photographs (pp. 53–55) was kindly supplied by Vauxhall Motors and demonstrates the assembly process of the Bedford CF in the factory. The CF body panels are held in place with jigs in preparation for welding, and, once assembled, are carried on hoists to the paint section.

A completed red Bedford CF delivery van being driven
off the production line to the holding park outside.

9

Bedford Auto-Sleeper
various models (CF)

The First CF model to be released by Auto-Sleepers was a rising-roof camper van using an internal layout that had proved so popular on their Commer model throughout the 1960s. This model was available as a 4/5-berth with a double bed made up from the dinette seats, two single bunks in the raised roof section and a child's bed in the cab area. The example seen here, WYB 570M (1.8ltr petrol), was the author's everyday transport for some time, pictured in front of a Breton longere *property in France.*

BEDFORD CF AUTO-SLEEPER (RISING ROOF MODEL)

One of the most respected names in the motorcaravan industry, Auto-Sleepers, have been producing high-quality models since the early 1960s from their base in Willersey, Worcestershire, and the Bedford CF became their first new model for a decade, although there was to be no innovative design on the Bedford base; instead, they stayed with the tried and trusted layout which had proved so popular on the Commer conversion. On opening the twin rear doors of the Bedford one was met by almost a carbon copy of the Commer layout. Due to the tremendous following that the Bedford marque had gained over the years, the CF Auto-Sleeper quickly established itself as a favourite with buyers. The first Bedford models were based on the CF18

with the 1759cc petrol engine; the 22cwt model was soon added with the more familiar 2.3ltr petrol engine. The average price of a standard CF-based Auto-Sleeper in 1975 was around £2,500. The list of optional extras had by then grown to include brake servo, steering lock, automatic transmission, chemical toilet, gas tap and fire, flyscreens, a carpet in rear, a roof rack and an electrical water pump in place of the foot-operated device.

The trusted layout offered on both the Bedford and the Commer base was also used in two other vehicles, notably the Mk.I and the Mk.II Ford Transit (Auto-Sleepers produced very few of these) and the Leyland Sherpa, released in 1975. The Sherpa-based model became a big seller indeed. The conversion on this Leyland offering did differ slightly from their standard layout, however. Because the Sherpa was not as wide as

the Bedford, the Commer or the Transit, it was unable to accommodate a double transverse bed. Instead, the sleeping arrangements were altered slightly to give two full-length, single beds, making use once more of the dinette seats, and this time the two cab seats which reclined to lie flat. This Auto-Sleeper model underwent detailed modifications and improvements throughout production and finally became the Utopian model when it was fitted with the redesigned rising roof and combined GRP luggage rack. The Utopian and its high-top stablemate, the CX200, continued in production until the mid 1980s, by which time the Talbot Express had become the base vehicle of choice for many converters.

It may not have escaped your notice that all the conversions offered by Auto-Sleepers up to this point were panel-

ABOVE: Auto-Sleepers continued to offer their rising-roof example on the CF well into the 1980s (then as the Utopian), and seen here is a 1979 example with revised roof capping, which had a small luggage rack incorporated in the front roof section.

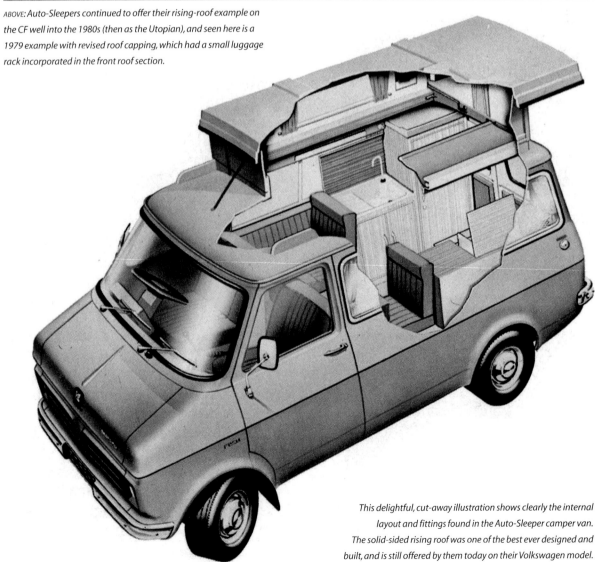

This delightful, cut-away illustration shows clearly the internal layout and fittings found in the Auto-Sleeper camper van. The solid-sided rising roof was one of the best ever designed and built, and is still offered by them today on their Volkswagen model.

Interior view of the CF Auto-Sleeper with rear doors held open and the rising roof in the lowered position. No space was wasted in this model; note the fitted cupboards on the rear doors, which made use of the door cavity.

The hand-crafted cupboards in all their glory; this is the kitchen facility with centrally located gas hob/grill, cutlery drawer below and more storage below that. The cupboard to the right of the cooker was fitted with a shelf for further storage and the cupboard door at the far end is where the refrigerator was housed.

Opposite the kitchen/cooker unit was the sink/drainer unit with a large cupboard below and hinged worktop. The unit alongside the sink/drainer is the wardrobe, complete with clothes rail.

RIGHT: Another view of the sink and wardrobe units, with one side of the dinette/double bed at the far right. This inward-facing seat could be altered for travelling, allowing the rear passengers to face forward when one of the cushions pictured became a backrest (no seat belts were fitted).

van motorcaravans with an elevating roof. This was to change in 1977, when, after seventeen years of conversion; the company released their first coach-built example, the CB22.

AUTO-SLEEPER BEDFORD CB22

Everything that the company had learnt from many years of conversion work was carried forward to the new coach-built model. Auto-Sleepers used such slogans as 'five-star luxury on wheels' to describe their latest offering. In fact, the sales brochure for this model claimed that it was 'such a complete specification – there are no optional extras', which really did say everything about the new CB22. There was certainly nothing innovative about the exterior styling – it was very square with a traditional Luton area above the cab, although the roof of GRP manufacture was a one-piece system, thereby reducing the possibility of leaks at a future date.

The CB22 was constructed by using the established method of cladding a timber frame with aluminium panels; the body was insulated with polystyrene throughout, including the floor. For this model the company used the CF250 base with the 2279cc petrol engine fitted as standard; a GM 2064cc diesel was available as an option. The transmission was the familiar four-speed with floor-mounted gear change. The GM automatic box was another option available, together with an overdrive gearbox on the petrol engine.

Access to the coach-built living area was by a single rear door; a folding access step was incorporated below the entrance door. As with the Auto-Sleeper panel-van conversions, the layout was similar, but on a grander scale, a toilet/shower cubicle had also been fitted into the coach-built proportions. The furniture was placed once more along the internal walls, but this time a refrigerator was fitted as standard, as was a full cooker with

This is a view of the Auto-Sleeper rising roof in the closed position, as seen from the rear of the vehicle. To operate it, the two chrome handles on the centre piece of wood were pushed up, leaving the two side flaps to be lifted into position. Two plastic pole holders can be seen at the bottom of the picture (there were two at the other end) and the two roll-away bunks are seen at the right and the left of the picture.

The same roof in the closed position, but from a slightly different angle; in this picture one end of the aluminium bunk pole can be seen top left. Long side windows were fitted to either side, with sliding sections for ventilation on site.

The rear end of a CF Auto-Sleeper with the roof lowered; the fibreglass roof capping was fitted with a rubber sealing extrusion and the entire roof sits well with the external lines of the CF bodywork.

oven. Another feature added to this model was the gas boiler in order to supply hot water to both the sink and the shower. Two other additions not found in panel van models was a full cocktail cabinet with glasses and a floor-mounted gas fire.

Because of the coach-built dimensions, two full double beds were now available. One was made by the conventional method of using the dinette seats; the other was to be found in the large Luton area above the cab; access to this bed was by ladder. Just some of

the other features found in the CB22 and fitted as standard were: flyscreens to all windows, three opening roof vents, carpet throughout, five fluorescent lights, vented locker housing the gas cylinder, mains electrical socket, full complement of crockery and glass for four people and a large wardrobe. It was a most impressive list of standard features, and to this day this remains a highly sought after motorhome on the classic scene; it had the best use of internal space I have seen in a small coach-built example, giving the impression that you were actually in a motorhome of far greater dimensions. Putting the external box-like appearance to one side, the clever use of floor space within the living area of the CB22 was pure brilliance, and clearly designed by a motorcaravanner!

AUTO-SLEEPER CLUBMAN/SV100

The first Auto-Sleeper coach-built model, the CB22, had been an undoubted success for the Willersey-based company, but in November 1980 the CB22 was superceded by the SV100 model, again based on the Bedford CF. This was a very different design concept to the previous CB22, as it was an all-GRP monocoque-bodied motorhome, unlike anything else on the market at that time and was the work of leading stylist William Towns of Aston Martin fame. It was based on the Bedford 250 chassis with luxury cab, fitted with the 2279cc petrol engine as standard (a 2260cc diesel unit was an option).

The SV100 was a side-entrance model with the kitchen facilities situated along the rear of the living area. This kitchen comprised a stainless-steel sink/drainer, two-burner hob with grill and oven, hot and cold running water supplied from the gas boiler, fold-back worktops, storage cupboard and a large window above the kitchen, giving the maximum light for food preparation. In the rear corner of the vehicle was a full-height washroom with vanity mirror, hand basin, electric strip light and shower. Along the interior wall, immediately behind the passenger cab seat, was the wardrobe, gas storage locker, space heater and the refrigerator, with a wipe-clean worktop covering the refrigerator and gas storage locker. Above this were a pair of eye-level

RIGHT: The engine bay of the CF; on the CF range the engine was located half inside the driving cab (accessed via a cover) and half under the bonnet. The unit seen here is the fairly economical 1.8ltr petrol engine, though many preferred the 2.3ltr.

BELOW: Not your traditional looking CF Auto-Sleeper, but a much loved and admired survivor, this is 'Clarice' the camper owned by Dave and Mel, of Leicestershire. The bodywork has been finished in a gorgeous metallic finish of two-tone green, while the retro-fitted alloy wheels and chrome mirrors give a custom feel to a classic camper van of 1970s vintage.

cupboards and a strip light fitted at the base. Opposite these units (between the rear of the driver's seat and the washroom) was the dinette/double-bed area. The seating arranged for two people to sit and face the rear, and two facing the front, with a table in between for dining. At night these cushions (and backrests) were laid flat to form the double bed. More eye-level storage lockers were placed above the dinette/bed area and an additional double bed was situated in the over-cab area.

Other notable features of the SV100 included the large sliding side with tinted glass and built-in flyscreens, fitted roof ventilators, fitted carpets to the cab and dinette areas, five fluorescent strip lights, mains electricity hook-up and sockets, curtains to all windows, large capacity fresh and waste water tanks and an external roof rack with built-in access ladder. A nice added

Graphic on the side of Mel and Dave's CF proudly proclaims that this is Clarice the camper, while another graphic on the side states 'Saved from the grave by Mel and Dave', in honour of the fact that she really was moments from being crushed.

touch in all Auto-Sleeper models for many years was the addition of a full crockery set as standard. All in all, the SV100 was a comprehensively equipped motorhome, extremely well built and very well designed. It was thus little wonder that it won the title of 'Motor-caravan of the Year' from 1981 to 1983.

The price of an SV100 Auto-Sleeper in March of 1983 was £12,261, including

Bedford Auto-Sleeper, various models (CF)

Not only was Clarice saved from a scrapyard and fully restored during the 1990s, but owner/mechanic Dave then rebuilt the CF Auto-Sleeper again quite recently to an even higher standard. It is seen here on the right (alongside a CA Dormobile) being exhibited at the Classic Motor Show at the NEC in 2008.

BELOW: One of the finest coach-built models produced by Auto-Sleepers, this is an excellent example of their CB22.

RIGHT: This particular example, dating from 1977 and owned by Ken and Geraldine Walker of Worcestershire, must be one of the first CB22 models to have been produced. The coach-built CB22 on the CF chassis was the first such model to be released by Auto-Sleepers, who had built their reputation for quality upon the likes of Commer, CF, Transit and Sherpa rising-roof examples.

RIGHT: Interior view of the same model, as seen through the rear entrance door.

VAT. With some design tweaks and internal changes, the SV100 became the Auto-Sleeper Clubman, another top-selling Bedford model of the 1980s.

CLUBMAN

The external appearance of the Auto-Sleeper Clubman was almost identical to that of the earlier SV100 model, other than for alterations to colour and graphics. That William Towns design had proved to be highly popular with the buyers, so why change a winning formula? The major differences between the SV100 and the Clubman were internal. The Clubman retained the side-entrance door and the kitchen along the rear wall, and the refrigerator was retained just inside the entrance door, the washroom, as in the SV100, was in the rear corner, but this is where the similarities between the SV100 and the Clubman came to an end: for the Clubman model the designers had altered the dinette area and done away with the two inward-facing seats located to one side of the vehicle. In the Clubman the designers had reverted to a far more traditional dinette layout featuring two bench-style seats to each side, directly behind the cab seats, although when travelling one could create two single forward-facing seats (unbelted). For dining an island-leg table was placed in the centre gangway, allowing four people to sit comfortably. This dinette became the double bed at night by utilizing the seat cushions and the backrests. Alternatively, the two side bench seats, together with fold-flat cab seats, could form two single beds. In order to create this dinette arrangement the design team had moved the wardrobe to a position alongside the washroom, with a thermostatically controlled heater placed at the base. The next internal change was to be found in the cab area, notably that the ready-made double-bed position had been cut away in the Clubman to allow direct, uninhibited access through from living area to the cab. But the space above the driving cab could still be used for a double bed by using a pull-out board system.

Another view of the CB22 interior with the dinette/double bed and cab area in view; the hole in the centre of the floor aisle is for the island-leg dining table.

Bedford Auto-Sleeper, various models (CF)

LEFT: A close-up shot of the dinette base in order to show that, as well as using the seats in the inward-facing position for dining, this wooden base section could be altered in order to allow the rear passengers to face forward when travelling, though no seat belts were fitted at this time.

RIGHT: The cooking facilities in the CB22 are located on the right-hand side (when entering from the rear), as seen here, with the gas hob/grill in a central position, worktops on either side, ample cupboard space below and the refrigerator housed in the cupboard to the left of the cooker. The tall cupboard in the corner is the full-length wardrobe.

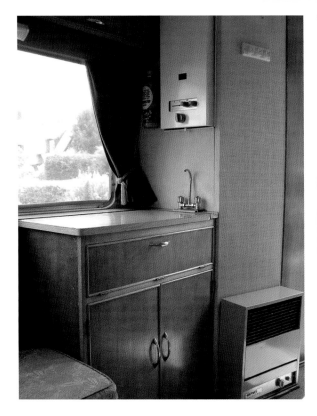

LEFT: The CB22 was advertised as the complete package, with no need to offer any optional extras, because it was so comprehensively fitted as standard. Here are just two reasons why – a gas water heater and gas space heater, two features often put on the list of options by converters in the 1970s, but not Auto-Sleepers. This is the unit opposite the cooker unit and contains the sink/drainer, plus the huge storage cupboard below.

ABOVE: The same unit, but this time with the worktop lifted.

RIGHT: *Storage units were not confined to floor-mounted examples, as this picture illustrates. Above the cooker unit was a built-in cocktail cabinet (supplied with glasses) and eye-level cupboards, all along the roofline on both sides of the interior.*

LEFT: *One of the few non-original features in this particular example is the replacement refrigerator seen here.*

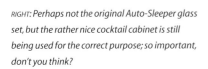

RIGHT: *Perhaps not the original Auto-Sleeper glass set, but the rather nice cocktail cabinet is still being used for the correct purpose; so important, don't you think?*

ABOVE: There is great attention to detail in the CB22 interior, like this chrome turnbuckle catch to keep the wardrobe door firmly in place when travelling.

LEFT: The original 'Carver' space heater located on the lower wall section between the sink/drainer unit and the washroom (washroom door visible to the right).

Seen here is the area above the cab (with curtains drawn), another double bed of ample proportions and ventilation skylight (in the central roof section).

LEFT: *Side view of the CB22 external bodywork, with exterior ventilator for the refrigerator, bold, coloured coach lines and large sliding window (fitted with flyscreens).*

ABOVE: *The exterior access hatch for the gas cylinders, located at the rear of the vehicle.*

BELOW: *Introduced in 1981, the William Towns-designed Auto-Sleeper SV100 was a fibreglass, reinforced body with appealing external appearance. Entry was by a side-rear door and there was an over-cab double bed, in addition to a double in the downstairs living area. This model, seen here alongside the rising roof SB45 Utopian, won the coveted title of 'Motor Caravan of the Year' in 1981–2 and 1982–3.*

Bedford Auto-Sleeper, various models (CF)

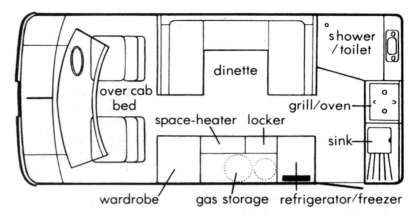

RIGHT: *Floor plan of the Auto-Sleeper SV100, based on the Bedford CF250 chassis, with rear-end kitchen facilities, corner washroom/toilet and a U-shaped dinette and wardrobe, refrigerator and gas storage opposite. The SV100 was powered by the 2.3ltr petrol engine as standard, with a 2.6ltr GM diesel unit as an option.*
BELOW: *The Auto-Sleeper SV100 was later given a revised internal layout and the Clubman model was born. The main internal difference between the two models was the fact that in the Clubman the U-shaped dinette to one side was replaced by two inward-facing seats, similar to those in the Auto-Sleeper rising-roof model.*

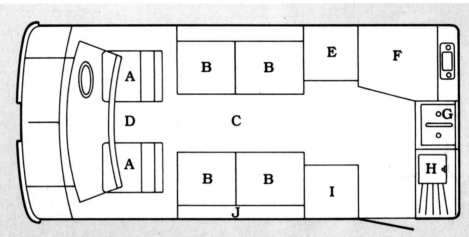

A. Fully adjustable luxury cab seats.
B. Dinette converting to two front facing seats.
C. Table.
A. and B. convert to two longitudinal single beds, OR
B. and C. convert to large double bed.
D. Cut-away cab with pull-out bed.

E. Wardrobe with thermostatically controlled heater below.
F. Shower/toilet compartment.
G. 2-burner grill cooker with oven below.
H. Stainless steel sink and drainer with cupboard below.
I. Refrigerator-freezer.
J. Gas storage with external access.

External picture of an early CF Clubman, which has obviously been well cared for; the beauty of this model is that the living area will not rust and rot due to the fibreglass method of manufacture.

ABOVE: This is the view through the side-entry door of the Clubman interior, with the kitchen along the back wall and the washroom/toilet in the far corner.

ABOVE RIGHT: A slightly different angle, this picture illustrates the full-height wardrobe situated alongside the washroom, the vanity mirror mounted on the door with a space heater below. Just to the left, inside the entrance, the refrigerator can be seen, the door of which is facing the kitchen.

RIGHT: This is the interior view of the rear when standing in the dinette area, with the kitchen at the rear end, the washroom/toilet to the left corner and further units to the right, with an extending worktop.

BELOW: The dinette seating used to form a large double bed; with the front cab seats folded flat the occupants have a choice of which way they prefer to sleep.

ABOVE: The area above the cab can hold yet another full-size double bed, or, alternatively, becomes a large storage area for bedding and the like when the vehicle is used as a two-berth.

Bedford Auto-Sleeper, various models (CF)

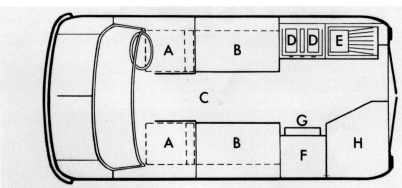

A. Fully adjustable luxury cab seats.

B. Dinette converting to two front facing seats. Alternatively, A and B convert to two longitudinal single beds, or B and C convert to a transverse double bed.

D. 2 burner/grill cooker with oven below.

E. Sink with refrigerator below.

F. Large wardrobe (cupboard with china above).

G. Optional heater.

H. Toilet compartment.

ABOVE: Dating from 1981, this was the other Bedford CF-based model in the Auto-Sleeper line-up, the CX200 high top. Based on the CF230 or CF250 chassis, the CX200 was released in order to fill a sales void between the coach-built SV100 and the rising roof SB45 Utopian model.

LEFT: A floor plan of the CX200 Auto-Sleeper shows it as able to incorporate a toilet compartment in one corner due to the fitting of a fibreglass high top. The dinette was capable of being transformed into a double bed or two longitudinal single beds. This model had such standard features as an oven, three-way-operation refrigerator and in-built freshwater tank.

10

Autohome/Motorhome CI/M-CI/A (CF)

From about 1972, this is a press picture for the CI Autohome, a new concept in motorhome design as its body was built independently of the vehicle chassis and attached once completed. Designed by Carl Olsen, the Autohome featured an over-cab double bed, dinette/double bed, kitchen facilities and a washroom/toilet.

CI/M AUTOHOME/MOTORHOME-BEDFORD (CF)

The Motorhome was a name first used by Caravans International (Motorised) Ltd back in 1966; in that year they unveiled the Sprite Motorhome, based on the Ford Transit, and that model ceased production in 1970. Caravans International had undergone a name change by 1974, and from that time had become 'CI Autohomes Ltd', and their Carl Olsen-designed Autohome model had evolved into the CI Motorhome Mk I. Once more the new Motorhome model was made available on the Bedford CF, Commer and Ford Transit chassis; the Autohome/Motorhome body represented a radical design and build approach for the south coast company. The Motorhome bodywork was constructed independently of the base vehicle, on a wheeled jig in the factory, and only mated to the Bedford, Commer or Transit vehicle once completed. The new construction technique was said to improve the build time, made far

better use of factory floor space and made export far more economical.

The story of the CI Motorhome is one of constant change, restyling and improvements. The original Mk.I version of the Motorhome was simply an evolution of the previously released (and very successful) Autohome model, first unveiled in 1971. As early as 1976 the company had already unveiled the Mk.II Motorhome, with detailed improvements over the Mk.I, but I will begin my description with a look at the Mk.II version, concentrating solely on the Motorhome body and not the base vehicle since the Motorhome was available on all three popular base vehicles of the period, the Bedford CF, the Commer and the Transit.

The Motorhome had a single rear-entrance door and a combined toilet compartment/wardrobe in the rear right-hand corner (viewed looking toward the driving cab). This combined unit had a bi-fold door system, which allowed for the creation of an extended area when using the facilities. It was

fitted with a drop-down wash basin, vanity mirror, ventilator and electric light. Alongside the toilet/wardrobe was a cupboard unit with fitted worktop; the refrigerator was housed in one side of this cupboard with shelving to the other side. On the opposite side was the kitchen area and this featured a stainless steel sink with drainer, two-burner hob and grill, together with an array of storage cupboards and drawers below. Eye-level cupboards were placed above the kitchen, giving yet more storage space. The internal layout of the Motorhome was quite traditional, with the dinette situated just behind the cab. The table, stored under the mattress in the over-cab area, could provide enough room for six people to dine in comfort.

At night the dinette converted into a double bed, and a double child's bed was to be found in the over-cab area, with the option that one adult could sleep in this area in place of two children. CI Autohomes did, in fact, fit an extension flap to the base of the over-cab bed in order to accommodate two

Autohome/Motorhome CI/M-CI/A (CF)

This artist's cut-away illustration shows clearly the interior features of the Autohome model.

BELOW: The Autohome fairly quickly transformed itself into the CI Motorhome; externally the two models were almost identical.

adults, but it remained a rather confined space in which to manoeuvre. The metal safety rail placed along the outer edge of this upstairs bed doubled as a ladder. Further features of the upper bedroom were a long window to the front, with a curtain and an electric light. An additional stretcher bunk could be ordered to fit transversely into holders and across the dinette bed. There was also the option of a similar bunk for the driving cab.

Some other standard features of the Motorhome Mk.II included exterior access to two gas bottles in the rear, a mixture of both carpet and vinyl flooring, two fluorescent lights, on-board water tank, curtains to all windows, upholstered seating in the dinette/lounge and an opening, roof-mounted ventilator. All the cupboards in the Motorhome were finished in a wood-effect laminate. This model was very light inside due to the good selection of rear and side windows, with the side windows having opening panels. Towards the end of Mk.II Motorhome

Artist's cut-away illustration of the CI Motorhome; by studying the cut-away drawings of both the Autohome and the Motorhome it becomes a game of 'spot the difference', the changes were minor.

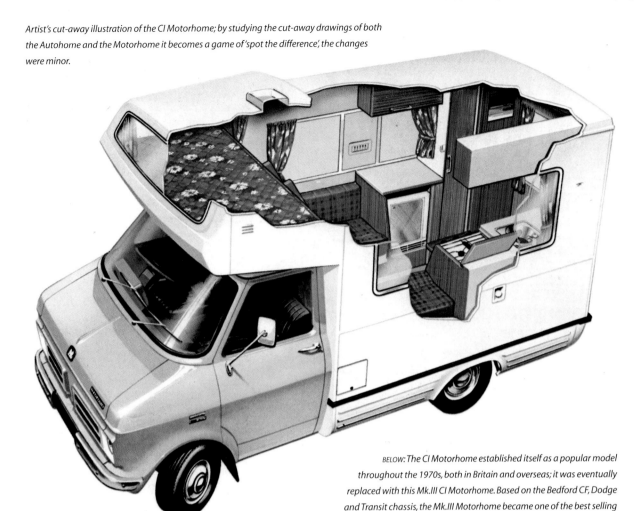

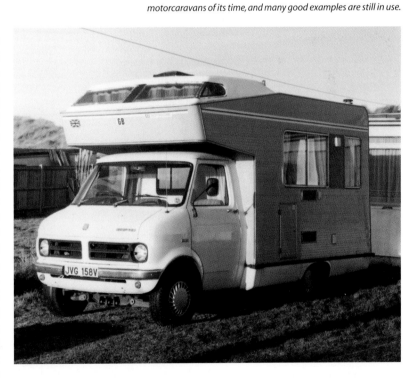

BELOW: The CI Motorhome established itself as a popular model throughout the 1970s, both in Britain and overseas; it was eventually replaced with this Mk.III CI Motorhome. Based on the Bedford CF, Dodge and Transit chassis, the Mk.III Motorhome became one of the best selling motorcaravans of its time, and many good examples are still in use.

production the wardrobe (now smaller) was moved along to give 80 per cent more room in the toilet compartment. At the same time some minor detailed changes were made to the external appearance. With regard to price, the CI Motorhome was listed as follows in 1975: the Bedford CF, £2,972; the Commer, £2,835 and the Ford Transit, £3,180.

By 1978 the CI Motorhome had been completely redesigned, it was also much larger than the previous model. Although the base vehicle options remained the same, both the Ford Transit and the Commer had been altered significantly. By now the Mk.II Ford Transit had been introduced and the Commer had been renamed the Dodge Spacevan. In the Mk.I and the Mk.II variants, the CI Motorhome had been the best selling coach-built motorcaravan throughout Europe; the launch of the Mk.III version would see the model consolidate its position.

The new Mk.III model retained the single rear-entrance door and the double bed in the over-cab area, but the internal layout had been altered considerably. Looking into the interior from the rear door, the toilet compartment remained in the right-hand corner. It was fitted with a tip-up wash basin and a wall-mounted cupboard as standard, the cupboard had sliding mirror doors and was fitted with a light above; both the

**The Bedford motor caravan.
All your holiday needs under one roof.**

This advertisement from the late 1970s makes reference to the fact that the Mk.III Motorhome was very well equipped in its standard trim.

cupboard and the sink were now of a beige colour. Situated next to the toilet and on the same side, were the dinette and the table. Although these were not in the usual position directly behind the cab, they were now just to one side of the living area, leaving a walkway into the driving cab. On the opposite side of the living area was the kitchen, with a wardrobe at the front end, just behind the passenger seat. Given that the kitchen took up the whole of one side interior wall, this was a spacious design feature and incorporated a huge worktop. Having previously owned a

ABOVE: *The Mk.III Motorhome was built to fit any one of three different base vehicles: the Ford Transit Mk.II, the Bedford CF and the Dodge (Commer).*
BELOW: *From its inception in the early 1970s, the Motorhome model was constantly updated and redesigned; seen here is the Mk.IV version on the revised CF base. An up-market version of this model was available at the same time with a much better standard specification and sold under the model name of Travelhome S.*

Floor plan for the later Mk.IV Motorhome; by this time, its builders, CI /M of Poole, had become Autohomes (UK) Ltd.

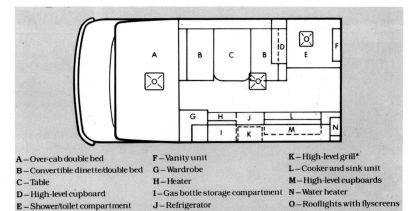

A – Over-cab double bed	**F** – Vanity unit
B – Convertible dinette/double bed	**G** – Wardrobe
C – Table	**H** – Heater
D – High-level cupboard	**I** – Gas bottle storage compartment
E – Shower/toilet compartment	**J** – Refrigerator

K – High-level grill*
L – Cooker and sink unit
M – High-level cupboards
N – Water heater
O – Rooflights with flyscreens
* Travelhome S only

Mk.III Motorhome, I can honestly say that it was one of the best interior layouts of any motorcaravan I have ever owned or used.

When sleeping, the dinette converted to a double bed and another one was to be found in the over-cab area. But on the Mk.III model this upper storey bed certainly was easily capable of sleeping two adults in comfort. Optional stretcher bunks were available for both the living area (near the dinette) and in the driving cab. The whole interior of the 1978 Motorhome was typical of 1970s design and colour. All cupboards were dark brown, with sidewalls in an oatmeal shade. The worktop was in a pale yellow colour, matching the front of the refrigerator. All curtains and seating upholstery were a mixture of brown, gold and beige patterned colour.

The CI Motorhome in its several model designations was undoubtedly one of the great sales successes of the 1970s, it sold in huge numbers both in Britain and on mainland Europe. It also remains one of the most distinctive coach-built models of the period, and the Mk.III version in particular with its external styling and gold body colour. The price for a Mk III Motorhome in 1978, based on the Bedford CF, was just under £7,000. A large number of examples from this period remain in use both in the UK and throughout mainland Europe.

ABOVE: There are many Autohomes' CF Motorhome Mk.IV models still in regular use, as this example on a Y-registration plate testifies. Note the revised CF cab.

BELOW: Even the earlier Autohome/Motorhome models produced by CI/M are still giving their owners hours of pleasure several decades later; seen here is one such example with a tear-drop caravan in tow.

11

Bedouin (CF)

CI/M (later Autohomes) of Poole produced some excellent motorcaravans over the years based on a variety of chassis; this is a model introduced in 1970, the Bedford CF Bedouin. Built in the traditional coach-built manner of aluminium panels applied over a wooden frame, the Bedouin had a fibreglass rounded front section. No colour choice options were available on this model – with the name Bedouin it had to be finished in sandy-gold.

The Bedouin coach-built model based only on the Bedford CF was released by CI/Motorised in 1970. At the time of its unveiling to the public the company were already producing two highly regarded coach-built models, the Transit Sprite and Commer Highwayman. The Bedouin and its stablemates were constructed in the traditional coach-work tradition of aluminium panels over a wooden framework.

Based on the Bedford CF 22cwt chassis-cab with the de-luxe cab, the entrance to the living area was via a rear entry, single door. In external appearance the Bedouin wasn't too dissimilar to the Commer Highwayman. The interior finish was also similar to that of the 1970s Highwayman model with wood-effect surfaces, a dinette that converted to a double bed, and the long seat/settee near the rear also converting into an extra bed.

On entering the Bedouin from the rear door, a full-length wardrobe was positioned at the right-rear corner, with the kitchen facilities running alongside it. The kitchen featured a sink with draining board, a two-burner cooker with grill, optional refrigerator and storage cupboards both at eye level and beneath the cooker unit. Covering both the cooker and the sink was a split worktop, allowing either the cooker or the sink to remain concealed at any one time. When both worktops were raised, the only food preparation surface available was the fold-down flap, which concealed the grill. When the optional refrigerator was purchased, this was positioned under the sink unit. Water was supplied to the kitchen sink by an electric pump, from a 16gal/72ltr underfloor tank.

On the opposite side to the kitchen was a long upholstered seat, ideal for daytime lounging, which would convert into a double bed in the evening. Beneath this was a large storage area. Forward of both these side-mounted features was the dinette area, which again had upholstered seating and a free-standing table; this area converted to another double bed with further storage beneath it. These dinette seats could also be transformed into two forward-facing seats, although without the addition of seat belts/lap restraints

at this time. Above the driving cab in the Luton area was additional storage space. Fitted above the dinette was a transverse rollaway bunk; this could be rolled up and held with straps below the Luton area when not in use.

The living area of the Bedouin was double skinned and fully insulated, ventilation was provided by an opening roof-light and large sliding windows to either side. Three transistorized fluorescent strip lights at ceiling height provided lighting. Floor covering in the Bedouin was hard-wearing vinyl, and brightly coloured curtains were fitted to all windows. The gas bottle was located beneath the floor and accessible only from the exterior. The optional extras on this model were limited: a refrigerator, a flyscreen and a sealed-lid chemical toilet (this was housed at the base of the wardrobe).

Much to the annoyance of some buyers, the Bedouin was available in one only colour; this was a shade of sand/gold (no doubt to match the Arabian model name). The whole of the roof area was painted in off-white.

Artist's cut-away illustration of the Bedouin, showing all its
internal features and fitments.

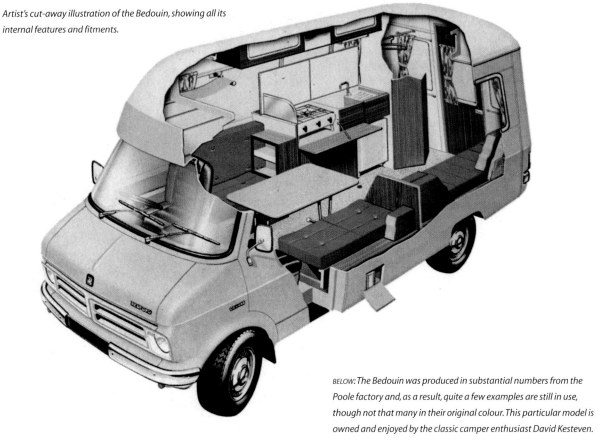

BELOW: *The Bedouin was produced in substantial numbers from the
Poole factory and, as a result, quite a few examples are still in use,
though not that many in their original colour. This particular model is
owned and enjoyed by the classic camper enthusiast David Kesteven.*

Bedouin (CF)

ABOVE LEFT: The Bedouin was a rear-entry model with the door in the rear centre of the vehicle, seen here. Along the rear side was a full-length settee, which had an extending base, allowing it to be transformed into a double bed.

ABOVE RIGHT: In this picture the long settee has been made into the double bed, and it will be noted that David has reupholstered the foam to match the exterior colour of his Bedouin.

The dinette area just behind the cab seats has an inward-facing, bench-style arrangement with a free-standing table in the centre. The cab seats seen here are non-standard fitments.

The price of a Bedford Bedouin when it was released in January 1970 was £1,458.5s.

It should be noted that the original water tank on this model during early production was of 12gal capacity (as compared with the later 16gal), and the electric water pump was also a later addition; early models had a foot-operated pump. One point worth mentioning in relation to the Bedouin was the fact that it was the first coach-built model ever released by CI/Motorised on a Bedford. Previously they had used only the BMC, the Commer and the Ford Transit bases for coach-built models. A little over halfway through the decade, the Bedouin was deleted from the catalogue, but the model name would reappear some years later.

Some months after the Bedouin was released, Wilson's the motorcaravan dealers in London, offered a modified version of it with the name Wilson's Bedouin Executive GT. The modifications and extras added nearly £500 to the list price quoted by CI/Motorised. The modifications made by Wilson's included heavily tinted black windows (not in the cab area), power brakes, a carpet, a push-button radio, eight-track stereo system (or portable TV option) and a GT engine conversion. A refrigerator was fitted as standard to the Executive GT model, together with a fire extinguisher.

The GT engine conversion was simply the addition of a twin-choke Weber carburettor, higher compression ratio and revised air induction. One of the most notable external differences between the standard model and the Executive GT was the matt black front grille and headlamp surrounds; this was all colour-coded on the standard model.

RIGHT: The dinette seats have been arranged to form a double bed, thus giving the Bedouin two double beds, plus the room for one or two small children in the area over the cab.

ABOVE: In the rear corner of the Bedouin (to the side of the rear door) is the toilet/washroom fitted with a chemical toilet and drop-down wash basin, ventilated with frosted glass windows.

RIGHT: Side view of the Bedouin interior, with worktops closed down over the sink and cooker, and the eye-level storage cupboards in view, and an over-cab area for either storage or a child's bunk.

ABOVE: Long-time Bedouin owner and Bedford enthusiast Eddie Dewe is the proud possessor of the example seen on the left, sheer heaven for fans of the griffin marque, with a CA in the centre and a vintage Bedford bus on the right.

RIGHT: Eddie travels all over the country in his Bedouin in order to display his classic motorcycles; he has modified the front passenger seat and the dinette seat seen here, and for a very good reason ...

BELOW: ... this is that he can fit his classic bikes into the Bedouin and secure them for travelling in the space once occupied by the passenger seat; a BSA trike is in residence here.

The Bedouin model name was to make a reappearance in the CI Auto-homes line-up at the beginning of the 1980s on the revised Bedford CF chassis. This time the company utilized their existing Highwayman body shell, as fitted to the Leyland Sherpa chassis, and revamped the interior design. The later Highwayman body did sit very well on the revised CF base vehicle and was well received by buyers at the time. In addition to the standard Mk.II Bedouin, Autohomes also released a limited edition version (with extra features included) in 1981, which they named the Bedouin LE; this was priced at £11,600.

ABOVE: *The Dormobile Land Cruiser based on the Bedford CF chassis, and looking magnificent while on display at a classic vehicle event. The Land Cruiser was an updated redesign of the earlier Debonair Mk.II, also on the Bedford CF.*

Rear view of the same vehicle, with beautifully curved, fibreglass, moulded bodywork; entry into the Land Cruiser was by the single door at the rear with a top-opening window.

Land Cruiser (CF)

12

LAND CRUISER-BEDFORD CF DORMOBILE

The Land Cruiser featured in this chapter is the model that was produced by Dormobile during the 1970s, a revised version of their 1969 Mk. II Debonair. I highlight this point simply because there were other models given this name: one in the 1950s and a previous Dormobile model based on the BMC 250JU high-top van in 1966 (though for that model of Dormobile the name became one word, 'Landcruiser'). To confuse matters even further, Dormobile also gave the name to their Leyland 20 motorcaravan of the mid 1960s.

An artist's illustration depicting a cut-away view of the Land Cruiser interior.

When entering the vehicle there is a long settee on the left-hand side and an ingenious hinged system utilizes the backrest of this seat in order to form a pair of bunk beds, as seen here.

The first Land Cruiser based on the Leyland 20 was not a great commercial success, but when the Bedford CF was released the Land Cruiser name was reinvented, and suddenly Dormobile had yet another popular model on their listing. The new Bedford–based Land Cruiser was first seen at COLEX (the Camping and Outdoor Leisure Exhibition) in 1971. Within a couple of years it had become very popular; I shall therefore describe the Bedford version of the Land Cruiser, of about 1973. The Land Cruiser was based on the 22cwt CF chassis and was powered by the 2.3ltr petrol engine. This was another Dormobile model, which was a one-piece GRP moulding but retaining the metal cab of the Bedford CF. The GRP moulding did, however, run the full length of the vehicle top, front to back with the low profile moulding over the driving cab also being of a GRP material.

Entrance to the Land Cruiser was through a one-piece glass-fibre rear door, glazed at the top; access to the living area was also possible through

the driving cab. When viewing the interior through the rear door, one saw a toilet compartment in the right-hand corner, although the toilet itself was not supplied as standard. This compartment was fitted with a bi-fold door, which meant that the compartment could be extended slightly when in use for privacy purposes. The only drawback with this toilet compartment was that it had to double as the wardrobe. Situated next to this, on the same side, was the well-equipped kitchen area. It consisted of a two-burner hob with grill, storage units below and a sink alongside the cooker. A refrigerator was situated below the sink, which was a standard fitment on this model. Water was pumped electrically to the sink from a 12gal tank mounted under the floor of the vehicle. Eye-level storage lockers were situated over the kitchen unit, but these were not repeated on the opposite side.

Opposite the kitchen and toilet compartment was a long, well-upholstered bench seat with matching backrest (the backrest was of a Pullman type and was used in the bed setup); this ran to a point level with the end of the refrigerator on the opposite side. Turning one's attention to the dinette area, this was a piece of typical Dormobile ingenuity. In addition to the two seats in the driving cab, there were also two forward-facing seats directly behind these. These two seats could be altered to form two inward-facing seats for dining (bench style), with the addition of a laminate-topped table. With the seating arranged in this configuration, there was, in effect, a length of seating running from the rear of the vehicle to the rear of the cab passenger seat.

TOP LEFT: Further storage lockers are located above the kitchen unit, all the furniture in the Land Cruiser being faced with a wood-effect laminate with white plastic edging and handles.
MIDDLE LEFT: Small storage area for table and other artefacts just above the cab.
BOTTOM LEFT: Plastic sink and drainer situated alongside the cooker with refrigerator below; both sink and cooker had hinged worktops.

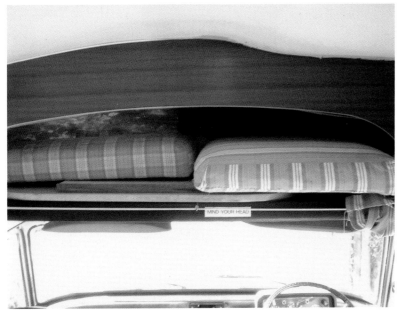

The sleeping arrangements once again made use of the dinette seating; this was kept in the dining configuration with the table forming the bed base, with the back cushions then placed over the table to complete a double bed. Bunk beds were quickly made up in the rear utilizing the long seat opposite the kitchen. The Pullman-style backrest of this seat could then swing up to form the upper bunk, with the assistance of two metal tubes; a detachable safety rail was supplied for the upper bunk as standard. This clever design meant that the floor space near the kitchen was clear and the toilet was still accessible throughout the night. There was the option of a stretcher bunk for a child in the cab area, and the area above the driving cab was quite large and suitable for storing large items or bedding.

Other standard features of the Dormobile Land Cruiser were a vanity mirror situated on the wardrobe door, a lift-up roof ventilator, a ceiling-mounted electric light, a fully insulated GRP body, vinyl flooring, curtains to all windows and a recessed gas bottle cradle below the vehicle floor. Interior cabinets were of a sapele veneer laminate.

The Land Cruiser was a popular well-equipped motorcaravan and remains very popular on the classic scene today. Owing to the glass-fibre rear bodywork, quite a number of models have survived and remain in regular use today.

When the Land Cruiser was first released in 1971 it was priced at £1,650, by 1972 it had risen to £1,994. In the aftermath of VAT introduction in 1973, the price of the Land Cruiser (along with that of all models) increased considerably, and by 1975 the list price was £3,434.

13

Freeway *(CF)*

*The Dormobile Freeway was a panel-van conversion released in the early 1970s by the Folkestone company; it featured
their famous rising roof, with its candy-stripe material and fibreglass luggage rack built on to the front section of the roof.*

The whole issue of Martin Walter Ltd
and the name Dormobile may appear
confusing to many. In actual fact the
matter is quite straightforward: Martin
Walter Ltd of Folkestone devised the
name 'Dormobile' to describe their utility vehicles during the 1950s, and the
name later became synonymous with
motorcaravans throughout the country. This began to happen to such an
extent that a motorcaravan in general
was being referred to, quite wrongly, as
a Dormobile. A Dormobile motorcaravan
was only genuine if produced by the
Martin Walter factory, it was a 'brand'
name. However, as with all major companies that trade over a large number

of years, there were inevitable changes
in both management and structure.
Such was the case with Martin Walter.
The Dormobile brand name did eventually become Dormobile Limited and
was then a member of the giant Char-
ringtons Group. The new company
emblem, a blue letter 'D', was designed
to represent the famous Dormobile
side-lifting roof.

The company switched its best selling
model names Romany and Debonair
from the Bedford CA to the Bedford CF
in 1969, to coincide with the release of
the new CF range of light commercials.
Both models evolved fairly quickly, the
Debonair becoming the Landcruiser

and the Romany became the Freeway.
In this chapter I focus on the highly successful panel-van conversion, with the
famous Dormobile rising roof, the Dormobile Freeway. There was a Freeway
model from 1973, based on the Ford
Transit 90 van (not described here), but
here I look at the Freeway based on the
Bedford CF 22cwt van from 1974.

The CF-based Freeway was a conversion of the 22cwt van; a petrol engine
was fitted as standard with a diesel
option available. This was a panel-van
conversion and so, naturally, the side-
hinged Dormobile roof was employed.
Fitted slightly forward of the GRP roof
capping was a contoured roof rack,

Freeway (CF)

Based on the Bedford CF 22cwt chassis, this is an artist's cut-away illustration of the 1973 version, which shows the rear dinette seats arranged as two separate units for forward travel. These seats could also be transformed into two bench-style seats for dining and also be used to form the double bed. Additional sleeping berths were housed in the raised roof section.

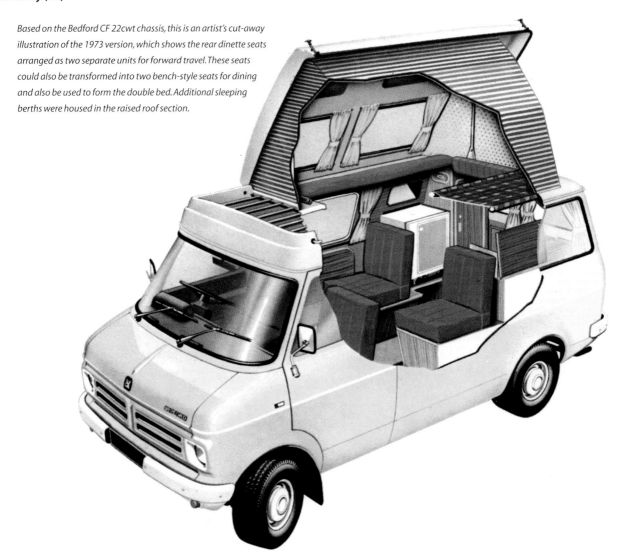

There are still quite a number of Freeway models remaining in regular use; this example is owned and cherished by Alan and Cath Houchen, of Leicestershire. Lovingly restored, the couple have deviated a little from the original colour scheme by adding a contemporary, two-tone red finish. With the roof in the lowered position, one can see that Dormobile achieved a rather pleasing design, and the GRP roof capping does not detract in any way from the classic lines of the Bedford CF bodywork.

LEFT: The same vehicle, this time with the roof in the raised position, and one can immediately see that the candy-stripe Dormobile material has been updated on this Freeway to an all-red colour in order to match the vehicle. Dormobile roof material is now available in a wide array of candy-stripe colour combinations, flower graphics and custom finish.

BELOW: The lovely clean and mostly original Freeway interior, on display in its full glory with traditional camper van layout consisting of units down each rear side, front dinette and central gangway.

again moulded in GRP. Entrance into the Freeway was by twin opening rear doors. Inside one saw a traditional panel-van layout with furniture positioned along each interior wall and the lounge/dinette just behind the driving compartment. These dinette seats (facing inward for dining) could be altered to face forward, thus giving four forward-facing seats when travelling (although, once again, in line with most panel-van conversions of this period, no rear seat belts were fitted). The clever Dormobile seating configuration allowed for the two front seats, together with the rear ones, to become two single beds as an option to the double converted from the dinette. The spacious rising roof housed two stretcher bunks, both measuring 6ft in length. A further option to accommodate another child for sleeping was a stretcher bunk within the driving compartment.

Viewing the interior from the rear doors, there was a kitchen to the right-hand side. This consisted of a two-burner hob and grill, sink unit with water pumped from a 12gal underfloor tank, and several storage lockers and cupboards. The units were finished in a wood-grain Melamine. Split worktops on top of the sink and cooker hinged upward to act as splash backs. Opposite the kitchen was a wardrobe unit and situated next to this was either a

The same view, but a closer shot showing slightly more interior detail; in this picture the table is seen erected for dining.

LEFT: An early example of the Freeway model based on the MKI Bedford CF. Recently restored with gleaming red paintwork, this example is well used throughout the year for both holidays and classic vehicle rallies.

BELOW LEFT: The seats immediately behind the cab seats have a triple use: they can be arranged as two individual, forward-facing seats for travel (no seat belts fitted), as two inward-facing dinette bench seats and the seats forming a double bed at night.

dresser unit or the optional refrigerator (placed above both of these options was a large vanity mirror). Two further storage pockets were built on to the interior of the rear doors. Seating in the Freeway was finished in a nylon and tweed fabric, and the floor covering was carpet laid over a Vynolay base. Even the cab area did not escape the Dormobile design touch, the dash being finished in a rosewood laminate. Curtains to all windows and fluorescent lighting complimented the remaining interior space.

The Freeway was available in a large number of body colour options from the Dormobile range. There were a couple of special edition Freeway models released during production, one being

Freeway furniture has a wood-effect laminate finish with white plastic edging; seen in this picture is the kitchen unit at the rear, which consisted of a two-burner gas hob/grill, sink, hinged worktops and an ample selection of storage cupboards below.

The refrigerator is located opposite the main kitchen unit, in a raised position; alongside this is the wardrobe in the rear corner of the vehicle.

The dinette seats with cushions arranged as the double bed, with further sleeping accommodation provided by two single bunks in the roof space.

the 'Pink Freeway' with a bright pink body colour, but if any now survive they have probably been repainted at some stage in a more conventional colour. Another special Freeway was the 'Tan Top' model. On this the GRP roof capping had a tan colour impregnated into it during manufacture (including the front roof rack). Also on this model, the traditional red and white candy stripes of the roof fabric were changed to tan, brown and white. Dormobile also offered a variation on the CF Freeway around this time named the Calypso. The roof was enlarged slightly on this model and the tan, brown and white roof fabric was retained from the Tan Top special. The interior was also revamped with the kitchen and the refrigerator switching sides. Other changes included a darker laminate finish to all surfaces and a distinctive flash decal to each side of the exterior. One of the most distinctive features of the Calypso was the tinted windows, designed to give the occupants more privacy. The cost of a Dormobile Freeway based on the Bedford CF in 1974 was about £2,500.

ABOVE: How about this as an alternative Dormobile roof on the Bedford CF? This design exercise in the early 1970s saw Dormobile construct an enormous, side-hinged version of their roof, with added metal support hoops and a large amount of extra roof material. The construction of the one-off roof is seen taking place here in the Dormobile factory.

LEFT: The finished roof atop a Bedford CF outside the Dormobile office building in Folkestone, the 180-degrees roof is seen supported by legs at each corner to take the heavy weight. It was done purely as a design prototype and was never put into production.

14

Glendale (CF)

This press release photograph dating from 1979 featured the Glendale 1000L model based on the Bedford CF, a traditional, coach-built example of aluminium panels applied over a wooden frame with large over-cab sleeping area and side-entry door.

KJ Caravans entered the British motor-caravan market during the mid 1970s with their Glendale models. Based in Hull, the home of British caravan manu-facturing, traditional construction meth-ods were used for the Glendale, with coach-built bodywork of aluminium panels over a wooden frame. Those early Glendale models were similar in style, both externally and internally, to the Advantura range, as the Glendale also had a side entrance door and rear dinette arrangement. The Glendale models were available in a variety of berths and were given model designa-tions thus: the 1000L (four-berth), the 2000L (six-berth), the 2500GL (four-berth) and the 3000L (six-berth). Origi-nally available on the Bedford CF, the Ford Transit and the Leyland Sherpa, the Glendale underwent many design changes in production throughout

the 1970s and 1980s. As production increased and time went by, the Glen-dale became available on several other base vehicles, including the Dodge, the Ford A-series, the Mercedes, the Toyota and the Volkswagen LT. Even some Tal-bot Express-based examples appeared during the late 1980s with completely restyled Glendale bodywork.

For an overview of the model I shall describe the four-berth example dating from around 1978 which was available on both the Bedford CF280 and the CF340 fitted with the 2279cc engine; this Glendale would have been desig-nated as the 2500GL model. Entrance to the living area was by a side door, and immediately to the left-hand side was the washroom/toilet. Facing the wash-room (rear of driver's seat) was the three-quarter height wardrobe and a three-way refrigerator at the base.

Alongside the wardrobe were the kitchen facilities, which included a two-burner hob/grill and a full oven with a hinged worktop over. Next to this was the stainless steel sink/drainer with sev-eral storage cupboards underneath and a worktop, which folded to one side away from the sink. A gas-fired water heater was situated on the wall above the sink/drainer supplying water to the sink and the washroom. An extractor fan was positioned over the gas hob and there were also eye-level storage lockers over the kitchen area. A side window above the sink/drainer gave excellent natural light for food prepara-tion, with an ample supply of electric lighting (throughout) for the evening.

A dinette was situated at the rear of the living area in a U shape, with an island-leg table provided for dining. Windows were placed at both sides and

RIGHT: This 1976 Glendale could possibly have been a prototype model, but what it does illustrate clearly is the ribbed aluminium panels of the bodywork; also note the single-glazed windows in the living area as opposed to the later 'smoked', double-glazed variety; an over-cab window is also missing from this example.

BELOW: Glendale models were available in a variety of berth options, from SWB to LWB. Seen here is a 1970s survivor still being put to good use.

BOTTOM: The same model as seen from the side; this view gives one a good impression of the total length – enormous! It features a rear dinette area, main units in a central position, further sleeping berths just behind the cab seats and more sleeping berths in the over-cab bed.

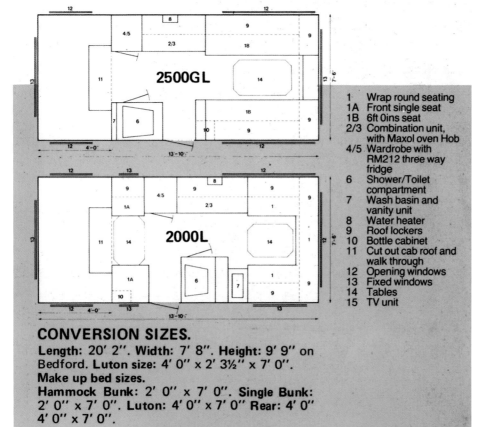

1 Wrap round seating
1A Front single seat
1B 6ft 0ins seat
2/3 Combination unit, with Maxol oven Hob
4/5 Wardrobe with RM212 three way fridge
6 Shower/Toilet compartment
7 Wash basin and vanity unit
8 Water heater
9 Roof lockers
10 Bottle cabinet
11 Cut out cab roof and walk through
12 Opening windows
13 Fixed windows
14 Tables
15 TV unit

CONVERSION SIZES.

Length: 20' 2''. Width: 7' 8''. Height: 9' 9'' on Bedford. Luton size: 4' 0'' × 2' 3½'' × 7' 0''.
Make up bed sizes.
Hammock Bunk: 2' 0'' × 7' 0''. Single Bunk: 2' 0'' × 7' 0''. Luton: 4' 0'' × 7' 0'' Rear: 4' 0'' 4' 0'' × 7' 0''.

ABOVE: These two pictures are views of the Glendale interior featuring the 2000L and the 2500Gl model variants. Glendales were well equipped, coach-built examples with a host of standard features for long-distance touring; all the furniture in the models of the 1970s had a wood-effect laminate finish.

LEFT: Floor plan layout for the popular 2000L and 2500GL Glendale examples.

This late 1970s press picture issued by Glendale of Hull is a side-on shot of the 2000L model.

in the rear of the dinette area, together with eye-level storage lockers all around. The dinette, in true motorhome fashion, also transformed into a double bed, and a further double bed was provided in the over-cab area, accessed by a ladder.

The specifications of the Glendale included a fully insulated (polystyrene) body and floor (foam) and an exterior comprising double-skinned panels. The interior furniture was constructed from teak vinyl on plywood, with the walls having a Shangtung vinyl on plywood. Teak Melamine worktops complimented the kitchen facilities, with the washroom/toilet walls clad in Ravenna vinyl-faced plywood. The interior of the Glendale was carpeted throughout and curtains were fitted to all windows, including the over-cab narrow window. Gas containers were housed in a separate locker, which was vented and accessed from the outside.

To identify some of the aluminium-clad motorhomes built during the 1970s can sometimes be a little tricky today since many have by now had the original decals and graphics removed to undergo a respray. During the past few

years I have probably been contacted by more owners of the old Glendale and Advantura models than of any other model, with the owners desperately trying to ascertain exactly what they have. Just to add to the confusion several converters building limited numbers of motorhomes at that time also used similar construction methods and exterior styling to the Glendale and Advantura models. During the course of my research for this book I discovered several old test reports written about Glendales, some of which only added to the confusion with regard to identification now. Ken Varey, who was the man behind KJ Caravans and the Glendale models, was quoted in one particular magazine as stating that quite often a customer would request changes to the standard Glendale models on offer, both internally and externally (this was a practice not confined only to Glendale). This is why some surviving examples may differ from those featured in old motoring publications, sales advertisements and sales brochures.

Here is a full Glendale model listing, from about spring 1982:

- Bedford CF250 Glendale 1000L, four-berth
- Bedford CF280 Glendale 2000L, six-berth
- Bedford CF340 Glendale 2000L, six-berth
- Bedford CF280 Glendale 2500GL, two+two berth
- Bedford CF340 Glendale 2500L, two+two berth
- Bedford CF250 Glendale 3000L, six-berth.

In addition to the Glendale models listed above, there was the release of another model in the late 1970s, the Glendale Major, which was based on the Bedford CF350. This was another six-berth model with a redesigned interior and the side entrance door moved further along the vehicle towards the rear. The Glendale Major retained the rear dinette/double bed but had a further dinette area (seating four) just behind the passenger cab seat. The Glendale Major had a price tag of around £8,000 in 1979; the prices for all the other Glendale models then started from £6,488.

KJ Caravans also produced a rising-roof model, as this 1980 advertisement testifies; the Glendale 500GL was well equipped and fitted with the Sherwood rising roof.

By 1984 the builders of the Glendale models, KJ Caravans, had become Glendale Motorhomes and sweeping changes had been made to the appearance of their models. This Glendale advertisement dates from 1984.

15

Jennings Roadranger (CF)

Chris Mountford of Forres is the proud owner of this real rarity, a Jennings Roadranger, based on the Bedford CF chassis. The Roadranger, built by J.H. Jennings of Sandbach, was just about the best luxury, coach-built example produced in Britain during the 1960s and early 1970s. Available initially on the Austin 152, Leyland 20, Commer and Ford Transit Mk.I, the Bedford chassis became an option in 1969 with the introduction of the CF. The great majority of Roadranger examples were built on the Ford Transit and the Commer base, so this particular CF survivor is a rare old beast indeed.

Sandbach, Cheshire was home to one of the most respected specialist coach-builders for over two centuries, J. H. Jennings & Sons. The company had produced their first motorized caravan as early as the 1930s, but at that time trailer caravans were proving to be far more popular than their motorized counterparts, and as a result Jennings did not re-enter the motorcaravan market for another thirty years. In 1964 Jennings unveiled their 'Roadranger' motorcaravans, luxurious hand-crafted models based on the BMC J2 chassis.

By the time the swinging sixties had arrived, it was the two grandsons of J.H. Jennings who lead the company, Derek and Tony. The Jennings motorcaravan was given the title Jennings Roadranger

and the first example was built on the Austin 152 base vehicle. It was constructed by using traditional coach-building skills and techniques: a hardwood frame was built, over which an aluminium skin was fitted. A one-piece GRP roof moulding was used, which had a distinctive curve to the front section, coming down over the cab. One other notable feature of Roadranger models was the large side flashing running the length of the vehicle (including the cab doors); this was always painted in a contrasting colour to that of the main vehicle body. Access to the Roadranger was by a single rear door, very heavy and somewhat reminiscent of the doors found on old train carriages, even the drop-down window in the top section of the door was a feature

borrowed from a train carriage design. Turning his attention to the interior, a prospective buyer of the period would have found this to be very familiar indeed. It was almost a carbon copy of the Paralanian model, first released in 1957, the reason being that Jennings had used the same designer and he obviously saw no point in tampering with an already excellent layout.

The Jennings Roadranger was available on a variety of base vehicles, with the interior design and layout differing little between one chassis and another; I shall therefore simply describe the Bedford CF Roadranger, given the topic of this book, but readers are reminded that the identical interior layout was available on the BMC J2, Commer 2500,

ABOVE: A view of the opposite side of the CF Roadranger, with the distinctive Jennings side flash visible and large side window with louvred centre section. This model has been retro-fitted with a more modern side sun awning/canopy.

RIGHT: Rear view of the Roadranger, showing that this was a rear-entry model with railway carriage-style door and drop down window. I can vouch from restoration experience that the Jennings rear door is very heavy indeed and was held with three hinges.

Leyland 20 (Standard Atlas) and the Ford Transit Mk. I.

The Roadranger was always intended as a luxury, two-berth model, although children's berths could be fitted as optional extras. Entering the Roadranger from the rear one would find a toilet compartment in the right-hand corner (rear) of the vehicle, this was fitted with a full-length single door. This compartment had a roof ventilator fitted as standard, together with a single wall-mounted light. Alongside this was the sink unit, which incorporated a stainless steel sink with drainer and a lift-up worktop faced with a laminate of wood-grain effect. To the right-hand side of the sink was a Whale hand pump for drawing water to the sink. Fresh water was kept in a 15gal tank stored under one of the dinette seats. A waste tank was also fitted underneath the vehicle

A further view of the
Jennings displayed for
outdoor dining; in this
instance table support cups
have been fitted to the side
of the vehicle, enabling its
dining table to be used
outside during fine weather.

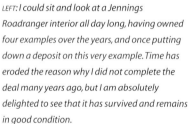

*LEFT: I could sit and look at a Jennings
Roadranger interior all day long, having owned
four examples over the years, and once putting
down a deposit on this very example. Time has
eroded the reason why I did not complete the
deal many years ago, but I am absolutely
delighted to see that it has survived and remains
in good condition.*

*BOTTOM LEFT: A view of the interior, this time
looking from the front to the rear, gorgeous
woodwork everywhere and a superb quality
finish, pure Jennings, with a kitchen divided
between each side, cooker one side and
sink/drainer opposite.*

rear with a drain-off tap. The remainder
of the sink unit consisted of a double-
door cupboard with shelves, and a
chest of five drawers next to that.
Above were eye-level storage lockers
with lift-up doors; these were fitted with
stay-put safety catches to hold them in
the open position. On the opposite side
from the toilet was a wardrobe of good
size; this contained a hanging rail,
storage shelf and a vanity mirror on the
inside of the door. Next to this wardrobe
was the kitchen unit, which had a full
cooker with oven, with the oven being
hidden behind twin-opening doors
when not in use. The refrigerator was
next to the cooker, but on early models
this was an extra and this space was
occupied by another storage cupboard, again with twin-opening doors.
A worktop was to be found over both the

TOP RIGHT: The dinette seats have been reupholstered since I last saw this CF Jennings, and the once luxury fitted carpet has gone, but I am sure that new owner Chris Mountford will bring the whole interior back to life with plenty of beeswax on the cabinet work. In this shot the table is set up for dining and the cab dividing screen is closed shut in order to separate the cab from the living area.

MIDDLE RIGHT: The Jennings is fitted with a full gas cooker consisting of a two-burner hob, grill and oven; twin doors at the front hinge out to provide access and the worktop folds to one side against the wardrobe wall. The refrigerator is situated alongside the cooker with a worktop over. The wardrobe can be seen in the far corner, though it looks as if some modification/customization has taken place in this area as all Roadrangers had a full-height wardrobe with a floor to ceiling door fitted.

cooker and the refrigerator/cupboard; again this was finished in a light wood-effect laminate. A catch on the side of the wardrobe held the worktop up when the cooker was in use. As on the opposite side, eye-level storage lockers ran across over these units, extending over the dinette area.

The dinette area consisted of two inward-facing seats, well upholstered with back cushions in matching fabric. The laminate top table was housed in its own storage locker with drop-down lid. This was located in a position under the over-cab storage area. In a smaller locker adjacent to this was a locker housing the wooden slats, which acted as the bed base. The slats were placed in recesses along each side of the dinette seat edge, and the seat bases and backs were used to form a double bed. The space above the cab was primarily for storage on the standard Roadranger, although a child's bed could be incorporated there as an option. In its standard form, this space was sealed with sliding wooden doors located at either side, with a vanity mirror in the centre. A single child's bed could also be ordered for the driving cab area as an option. A further option on the Roadranger was a partition between the living area and the cab; this could take the form of twin doors or a full lift-up wooden panel. If the two single-bed option was ordered then this panel was not available, since the beds used the cab seats for the two singles.

RIGHT: Opposite the cooker and the refrigerator is this sink/drainer unit containing a stainless steel sink, hinged worktops, storage cupboard behind twin-opening doors and a chest of five drawers. The door to the washroom/ toilet is seen in the far corner.

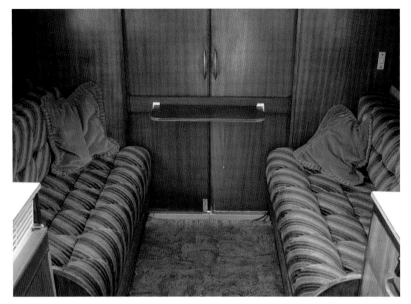

The dinette area with cab screen drawn closed; in this shot a small coffee table has been made by a previous owner to fit into the holders for the full size table, a nice addition when the full table is not required.

In order to make up the double bed from the dinette area seats one has to bridge the gap between the seats by inserting a series of wooden slats, these being housed in the table storage locker seen above the dinette, a clever design.

Aluminium-framed windows were installed on both sides of the living area (Venetian blinds were an extra for these side windows), the centre section of these was of the opening louvre type, and a large roof ventilator was fitted in the centre of the vehicle. Two electric lights were fitted as standard; these were fixed to the ceiling at either end of the interior, one switched from just inside the entrance door at the rear, the other from just behind the cab. Other notable features fitted as standard included a fire extinguisher, 12V power socket for accessories, storage compartment for two gas bottles, a point for a gas fire and good quality floor carpet in the living area. The list of optional extras on the Roadranger model was considerable, and included flyscreens for windows, stabilizing jacks at the rear, individual reading lamps, gas lights, a water heater and shower, chrome rear bumpers, a wash basin in the toilet compartment and an Aeon rubber suspension system. The standard interior wood finish was sapele, but an oak finish was available at extra cost.

Jennings always advertised the fact that they were willing to carry out any modifications required by customers and therefore some surviving models may differ from the description here. They were also willing to build Roadranger models on any base vehicle specified by a customer; it is known that Jennings Roadranger examples have survived based on such vehicles as the Land Rover, the Bedford TK and the large Mercedes chassis. With regard to prices, and using the year 1971 as an example, the Commer was listed at £2,098, the Bedford CF at £2,399 and the Transit at £2,393.

Remaining examples of the Jennings Roadranger based on the Bedford CF chassis are few and far between because the Commer 2500 and the Ford Transit were the most popular bases, and they were, of course, in production for some time before the CF Bedford was unveiled in 1969. Always a huge fan of the Roadranger models, I came close to purchasing a beautiful Bedford example some years ago, but my reasons for not buying the vehicle are now lost in the past. Thankfully, that example ended up in the hands of a real classic motorhome enthusiast in Scotland for several years, though it did re-surface on an internet auction site recently, and is now in the safe hands of Chris Mountford. Chris kindly supplied the Bedford CF Roadranger pictures used in this chapter, which clearly highlight the fabulous Jennings quality.

When Jennings ended production of the Roadranger motorhomes around 1972, they disappeared from the scene for some time, only to reappear in 1974 with a revised model sold under the name of the ERF Roadranger. This too was available on the Bedford CF and the Ford Transit, though few were built (a little over 200 examples), and the majority of those which were came on the MK. I Ford Transit chassis. I have only ever seen one example of the Bedford ERF Roadranger in the flesh, as it were, but it did appear in several Roadranger advertisements of the time, and it is certainly a model worth preserving if ever you are lucky enough to find one. The ERF version of the Roadranger featured a side-entry door and revised interior layout, but the quality was equally as good as the earlier Jennings Roadranger models.

The double bed is ready in a matter of seconds, I can testify to that having gone through the operation in a Roadranger many hundreds of times. Despite having to fit the wooden slats in place, it really is a fast manoeuvre.

Jennings/Bedford CF Roadranger

Chassis	Bedford CF 25 cwt. 1975 cc. petrol engine. Spare wheel and carrier. Heater and demister in driving compartment.
Extras	2524 cc. diesel engine. Power-assisted braking.
Dimensions	Overall: 16' 9" long. 8' 7" high. 6' 4½" wide.

Manufactured by
J. H. Jennings & Son Ltd., Sandbach, Cheshire.

This is the sales leaflet for the CF Roadranger model, about as rare as the real thing.

16 European Caravans Ltd, Advantura, Sundowner and Tourstar (CF)

As rare as hen's teeth, this is a Bedford CF Sundowner by European Caravans (Motorised) Ltd of Hull, about 1974. Constructed with a moulded fibreglass roof and aluminium side and end panels over a wooden frame, the Sundowner had a side-entrance door, as seen here; this example retains its original livery.

EUROPEAN CARAVANS LTD (MOTORISED)

European Caravans Ltd of Hull first entered the motorcaravan market in the late 1960s with their luxury Tourstar conversion on the Commer chassis (BMC derivatives were also available as the Sundowner). But the Commer Tourstar was an already established design, and a reincarnation of the much earlier Paralanian. By the early 1970s the company decided to concentrate their coach-building skills on the Bedford CF chassis, and adopted a very different design strategy from the earlier Commer Tourstar. The model names were retained, but this time there were no similarities between the new Bedford Tourstar and Sundowner and the old.

The new models were very similar in their external appearance, the difference being that the Tourstar had a rear-entry door and the Sundowner had a side-entry door. This was a large motorhome by British standards (18ft/5.5m in length) and utilized aluminium side and end walls with a fibreglass-moulded roof, incorporating an overhang above the driving cab. These were a pair of motorhomes that would not have been difficult to spot on a crowded campsite: not only were they quite large, they also had a very striking paint finish with bold coloured bands (over white) around the whole vehicle, which were either green, blue or an orange/brown combination. Both models were based on the CF250 LWB chassis and were fitted with the robust 2279cc petrol engine.

TOURSTAR

A radical exterior these models may have had, but the inside living space was very traditional with furniture constructed with oak-faced plywood. The bodywork of the motorhomes was insulated with expanded polystyrene, though the large, single-glazed side windows must surely have been responsible for quite a heat loss during cold spells. For internal description purposes I shall focus on the Bedford Tourstar with rear-entry door, as I believe that this was the most popular model option (though few examples of either remain today). Entering the vehicle one would find a washroom/shower on the right-hand side, fitted with a fold-up basin, shower attachment and plastic shower curtain. Opposite

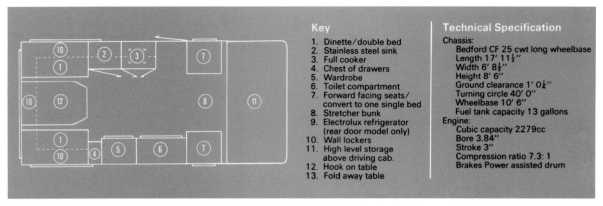

Key
1. Dinette/double bed
2. Stainless steel sink
3. Full cooker
4. Chest of drawers
5. Wardrobe
6. Toilet compartment
7. Forward facing seats/ convert to one single bed
8. Stretcher bunk
9. Electrolux refrigerator (rear door model only)
10. Wall lockers
11. High level storage above driving cab.
12. Hook on table
13. Fold away table

Technical Specification
Chassis:
 Bedford CF 25 cwt long wheelbase
 Length 17' 11½"
 Width 6' 8½"
 Height 8' 6"
 Ground clearance 1' 0¼"
 Turning circle 40' 0"
 Wheelbase 10' 6"
 Fuel tank capacity 13 gallons
Engine:
 Cubic capacity 2279cc
 Bore 3.84"
 Stroke 3"
 Compression ratio 7.3: 1
 Brakes Power assisted drum

Based on the CF 25cwt chassis, this is the floor plan of the Sundowner model; it is in fact the Mk.II Sundowner as a Mk.I version (different design) was available in the early 1970s based on the BMC 250JU chassis.

Identical in external body shape to the Sundowner, this is the Bedford CF Tourstar model; the major difference between the two models was the internal layout; due to the position of the entrance doors, Tourstar was a rear-entry model. The sister model, the Sundowner, can just be seen to the right of this picture.

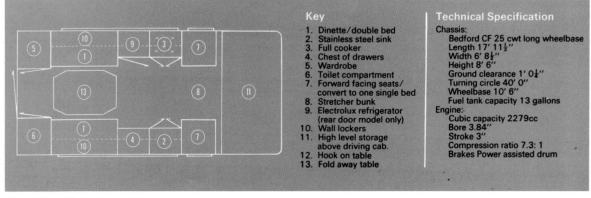

Key
1. Dinette/double bed
2. Stainless steel sink
3. Full cooker
4. Chest of drawers
5. Wardrobe
6. Toilet compartment
7. Forward facing seats/ convert to one single bed
8. Stretcher bunk
9. Electrolux refrigerator (rear door model only)
10. Wall lockers
11. High level storage above driving cab.
12. Hook on table
13. Fold away table

Technical Specification
Chassis:
 Bedford CF 25 cwt long wheelbase
 Length 17' 11½"
 Width 6' 8½"
 Height 8' 6"
 Ground clearance 1' 0¼"
 Turning circle 40' 0"
 Wheelbase 10' 6"
 Fuel tank capacity 13 gallons
Engine:
 Cubic capacity 2279cc
 Bore 3.84"
 Stroke 3"
 Compression ratio 7.3: 1
 Brakes Power assisted drum

Floor plan layout for the Tourstar CF.

Four noteworthy 'Europeans' to take you touring without a hitch

TOURSTAR SUNDOWNER, ADVANTURA and ADVANTURA LWB

European TOURSTAR & SUNDOWNER
4 berth. Well fitted for touring in style and built on reliable 2997 cc CF Bedford units.

European ADVANTURA
Two more models sharing basically the same specification as the other tourers. The Advantura being 4 berth and the long wheel base unit with room for six.

European Caravans (Motorised) Ltd.
is a member of the A Line Group

This 1970s advertisement from European Caravans of Hull shows the Sundowner and the Tourstar model being publicized alongside the Advantura models, though both the Sundowner and the Tourstar were fairly short-lived models once the Advantura had established itself, hence the rarity of those two models now.

this in the other rear corner was a full-height wardrobe with clothes rail and shelving, with the gas containers housed in a cradle in the base of the wardrobe. Adjoining both the washroom and the wardrobe were two inward-facing seats, which were fully upholstered with backrests, and these formed the dinette when the free-standing table was placed in the gangway. At night-time this dinette, with the use of a hinged board, formed a double bed of very good proportions. Eye-level storage lockers were situated above the dinette area on both sides of the interior, with electric strip lights fitted to the locker bases. Directly behind the front cab seats were two forward-facing, single seats, which also formed a single bed. Immediately above this single bed was the provision for a fourth single bed, this time of the stretcher-bunk type across the width of the vehicle, giving a total of six berths in all. The area above the over-cab section (on the standard model) was a contained storage unit fitted with two hinged doors, but at extra cost a further double bed suitable for children could be ordered in place of it.

Other features of the Tourstar included a pressurized hot and cold water system, underfloor freshwater tank, fitted carpets and curtains to all windows. The cost of the standard Tourstar model in the summer of 1974 was £3,245, though a long list of optional extras were available at additional cost.

The Advantura on the CF was available in both LWB and the SWB variant; a rather nice SWB model is seen here on display at a classic vehicle show.

ADVANTURA

The Advantura model was released toward the end of 1974 by European Caravans (Motorised) Ltd to complement their existing range of Bedford motorhomes, which included the Tourstar and the Sundowner. The Advantura was constructed from a wooden frame, which was clad in a mixture of both smooth and corrugated aluminium sheets; this method of construction had been used for years by the A-Line group (the owners of European Caravans) to build their holiday static homes/caravans.

The distinguishing features of the Advantura models were the side-entrance door and the rear dinette area. The Advantura was built on both the SWB and the LWB Bedford CF bases and

RIGHT: There was a considerable difference in size between the two Advantura models, as this LWB example clearly demonstrates; this model is owned by Bedford enthusiast Benson Langley and was being restored in 2009.

LEFT: The external appearance of the Advantura models was to change over time, with a revised styling and colour scheme, such a model is seen here in LWB format.
BELOW: A closer view of the revised Advantura styling and colour scheme, out had gone the plain white bodywork with bold brown stripes, in came a more subtle colour combination.

A rear view of the Advantura, which, in spite of some restyling, remained a side-entry model with a rear dinette/double bed layout.

Interior view of the rear dinette with the dining table in position; large windows gave occupants a good scenic view once camped on site, note the eye-level lockers all around.

water heater to supply water to both the basin and the shower unit. Along the side of the vehicle interior (behind driver's seat) were the kitchen facilities with sink/drainer, storage units, cooker and optional refrigerator. Storage lockers were positioned above the kitchen and fold-back worktops were fitted on top of the sink and the cooker. Long side windows were placed between the overhead lockers and the kitchen base units, giving adequate light for food preparation; a strip light was a standard fitting under the base of the overhead storage lockers.

The dinette area was situated at the rear of the living area and comprised two inward-facing bench seats with backrests, a table being placed in the gangway for dining. At night this dinette would convert into a double bed, and the seat bases provided a useful area for storage. A large window was fitted at the rear end of the vehicle and more overhead storage lockers completed this area of the Advantura. Facing the cooker and attached to the shower was the full-height wardrobe with hanging rail and shelf; a vanity mirror was fitted inside the wardrobe door. In this four-berth model the other double bed was in the over-cab area at the front, accessed by a ladder. The interior of the Advantura was fully carpeted throughout and curtains were fitted to all windows. Furniture and interior side walls had a wood-grain effect finish, with the ceiling having a smooth white finish. Opening roof vents were situated in the central section of the vehicle and in the over-cab area, with three electric strip lights fitted as standard in the living area.

In addition to this four-berth model there were also a five- and a six-berth option. This was based on the LWB Bedford CF chassis, and again had a side-entrance door and the familiar rear dinette. But this longer Advantura model had an extra dinette/single bed directly behind the front cab seats, as in the Tourstar model. With the rear bed and over-cab bed, this single berth gave a total of five berths, but with the addition of a stretcher bunk above the single a sixth Advantura berth was possible.

The price of the standard Advantura model at the beginning of 1975 was £3,316. Initially it was available only on the Bedford CF chassis, but later both

was available in four-, five- and six-berth layouts. I shall describe the popular four-berth model dating from 1975 based on the 22cwt Bedford CF chassis with the 2279cc petrol engine. This model had the entrance door positioned on the side, just next to the passenger cab door. On entering the living

area there was a washroom immediately on the right-hand side; this was lined with tile-effect boarding. In the standard form this washroom contained only a tip-up wash basin, electric light and a portable toilet, but for an additional payment a full shower could be fitted, together with a gas-fired

RIGHT: The kitchen area is well equipped, seen here is the unit along the side of the interior with cooker, extractor fan, stainless steel sink/drainer and copious amounts of storage area above and below, the finish of which was a dark wood-effect laminate.

the Ford Transit and the Volkswagen LT became optional bases. There were slight variations in the shape of the exterior bodywork of the Advantura during production, most notably to the over-cab design at the front. The rear end was also redesigned at one point, and the flat-ended finish was replaced with a section at the top rear which was 'flicked out' to resemble a fin. During the late 1970s the Advantura range was given an external facelift with some restyling of the bodywork, and at this time the colour schemes were also altered.

RIGHT: A slightly different view of the kitchen facilities with the refrigerator housed below the sink/drainer and a hinged worktop bridging the entrance door area.

BELOW: A press release picture from the late 1970s showing the interior of the Advantura Luxury 4, a model available on both the Bedford CF and the Ford Transit chassis, a well equipped motorhome with full oven, space heater, three-way refrigerator and washroom/toilet.

17

Brigand (CF)

ABOVE: The Bedford Brigand was a panel-van conversion by CI/Motorised of Poole, based on the CF 18cwt van with de luxe cab and fitted with their Parkestone rising roof; the revised 1974 model is seen here.

LEFT: This was the earlier version of the same Brigand model. Note the addition of a small window alongside the slider; this was omitted from later models.

The Brigand model became the first camper van based on the Bedford CF by CI/Motorised of Poole, and made its debut in 1969. A panel-van conversion, the Brigand was the sister model to the Commer Wanderer, and both were fitted with the Parkestone roof system.

The standard base for the Brigand was the 18cwt Bedford CF with the 22cwt base available as an option, both benefiting from servo-assisted brakes. The Brigand had the familiar panel-van interior layout, kitchen to one side and cupboards on the other, with the dinette converting to a double bed. This is the layout that had been adopted by designers of panel-van models (with rear doors) since the 1950s. It is straightforward, allows for an aisle in the middle of the van and dinette seating that can quickly be converted into a double bed. The Brigand was advertised as a four-berth model for four adults, but in reality the two bunks in the Parkstone rising roof would be more comfortable for two children. Access to the bunks in a panel-van conversion of this period was not easy, no matter which company carried out the work nor how well designed it may have been.

The word 'Brigand' as a model name may at first appear slightly strange given that a brigand is a roving outlaw/bandit, but the name is brought into context when one considers that

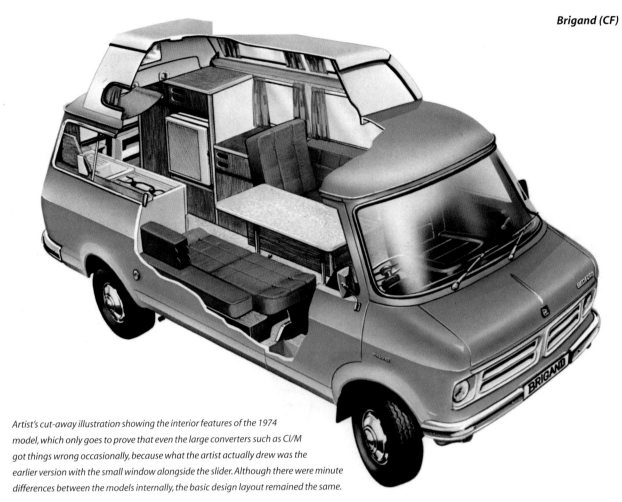

Artist's cut-away illustration showing the interior features of the 1974 model, which only goes to prove that even the large converters such as CI/M got things wrong occasionally, because what the artist actually drew was the earlier version with the small window alongside the slider. Although there were minute differences between the models internally, the basic design layout remained the same.

Press release picture of around 1972–73 of the Bedford CF Brigand, with its curved Parkestone rising roof. This roof was also fitted to its stablemate models, the Ford Transit Wayfarer and the Commer Wanderer.

the company had produced the High-wayman since 1958.

Viewing the interior through the rear double doors revealed the kitchen units situated along the right-hand side and ample storage units opposite. The kitchen consisted of a two-burner gas hob/grill, with a sink/drainer to the side. The space below the cooker and sink afforded the occupants a good deal of storage space, and if the optional refrig-erator was ordered, this was housed in a unit opposite the cooker. The worktop in the kitchen area was double-hinged, allowing either the cooker or the sink to be concealed beneath. Fresh water was delivered to the sink from an under-floor plastic holding tank via an electric pump. The furniture unit on the opposite side to the kitchen contained a small wardrobe, cupboard and two drawers, though these storage units were reduced somewhat if the optional refrigerator was ordered. Well-upholstered seating in the dinette area (either side of interior) could also be altered to form two forward-facing seats for travelling, and of course all of this seating was used to form the main double bed at night-time. Additional storage space was available beneath the dinette seats.

The gas bottle on this model was stored in a locker at floor level, inside the living area. The side windows on the Brigand were of the sliding design to aid ventilation and benefited from polished alloy frames. The window on the kitchen side of the vehicle ran the length of the living area, up to the rear of the cab. On the opposite side, however, the window was much smaller and situated in the area by the dinette.

The original metal panel to the rear was left in place in order to form the rear of the wardrobe and the refrigerator-housing cupboard. The sides of the van were fully insulated with fibreglass padding; the inner of the Parkstone rising roof was also insulated. Curtains were fitted to all windows and the floor covering was a hard-wearing vinyl. Lighting in the living area of the Brigand came from two fluorescent lights. The majority of Brigand models were either light blue or all white in body colour, but other options were available throughout production. Before the introduction of VAT in 1973 the Brigand carried a price tag of around £1,700; it ceased to be produced in the mid 1970s. By this time CI/Motorised had become CI/Autohomes and completely altered their construction technique for coach-built models, by then building the living 'box' independently of the chassis in their workshop and mounting the completed unit on to the base vehicle.

ABOVE: *Interior photograph of the same vehicle (see p.157). CI/M used the term 'luxury motor caravan' to describe the interior of their Brigand, I leave you to decide whether that was an accurate reflection of the fittings seen here.*

By the mid 1970s the Brigand had been transformed into the CI Autohomes Trailblazer; the interior layout was similar to that of the Brigand, but the Parkstone roof had been replaced by an altogether more modern rising roof operated by gas struts. This cut-away illustration is the February 1976 Trailblazer.

18

Pioneer (CF)

Built to special order for its owner Tony Willetts, this six-berth Pioneer was the first one to contain sleeping accommodation for six, based on a Bedford CF350 chassis. Tony collected this Pioneer from the Hull factory on 2 August 1979 and has been its single owner since; the Bedford has covered just 14,000 miles to date (summer 2009).

Pioneer Recreational Vehicles Ltd of Hull made the Pioneer range of coach-built motorhomes, an operation begun in 1979. David Hilton, the man behind the company, engaged the motorhome distributor Hayes Leisure of Darlaston to display his new range of motorcaravans at the Caravan and Leisure Exhibition at the NEC, though the 'range' at the time consisted of just a lone Pioneer 1204 model based on the CF280 chassis. This model featured a coach-built body of the over-cab design, with an outer skin of corrugated aluminium, a simulated cork finish for the interior walls and furniture with a dark walnut finish, all of which exuded quality according to an acquaintance of mine, Tony Willetts. He was present at the 1979 show and was very impressed by the Pioneer on

display, in his words it 'had something unlike any other coach-built displayed at that time'. But the problem was that, as a relatively new venture, Pioneer 'could not obtain chassis' quickly enough in order to satisfy the strong response from prospective customers. In May 1979 Tony had a meeting with Bill Hayes, head of the Hayes Leisure company, about obtaining one of the new Pioneer models, and Tony was told that it might be possible to have a Pioneer built and delivered by July, if Tony could provide Pioneer with the necessary Bedford chassis. Tony duly had a brand new Bedford CF350 chassis delivered to the Hull factory by mid June.

The only problem then was that the Bedford CF350, having twin rear wheels, was the largest CF chassis available,

and such a huge Pioneer motorhome was not part of the model line-up at that point. David Hilton of Pioneer was then persuaded to create a six-berth model, and thus the Pioneer ordered by Tony would be the very first six-berth Pioneer built by them. By August 1979 Tony's CF350 chassis had become a Pioneer 1206 and he collected the vehicle in person from the Hull factory on the day before they closed down for the August holiday.

Pioneer, according to Tony, had determined that its market would be 'high end', and they would include many items as standard equipment that converters then usually offered as optional extras. Here are some of the 'luxuries' fitted as standard to the Pioneer: double-glazed (tinted) safety

ABOVE: This shot shows the other side of the Pioneer and gives a better impression of its length; Pioneer models were entered by a side door, seen here.

LEFT: This Pioneer interior still looks like new today. Seen here is the kitchen unit featuring a gas hob, eye-level grill/oven, stainless steel sink/drainer and gas water heater and storage.

BELOW LEFT: A slightly different view of the same unit with the refrigerator below.

windows, pressure shower, gas heater, eye-level gas oven, two dining areas, pre-wired music system, strip and spotlights throughout, extra thick mattress bases, a range of customized fabrics and external gas locker. The Pioneer range quickly established itself with British motorcaravan buyers as a good quality, well-constructed model, which offered luxurious fixtures and fittings in a standard package. Within a couple of years Pioneer had built up quite a model line-up, giving buyers both a wide choice of berths and Bedford CF vehicle options; the full list by the early 1980s was:

- Pioneer 1004, Bedford CF250, four-berth
- Pioneer 1006, Bedford CF250, six-berth
- Pioneer 1206, Bedford CF280, six-berth
- Pioneer 1206, Bedford CF350, two-berth

- Pioneer 1002, Bedford CF250, four-berth
- Pioneer 1204, Bedford CF280, four-berth
- Pioneer 1204, Bedford CF350, four- and six-berth options
- Pioneer 1306, Bedford CF350L, berth option not specified but assumed to be six.

In the spring of 1982 these Pioneer models ranged in price from £9,874 for the 1004 four-berth, up to £13,082 for the 1306 model. One of the most popular models in the Pioneer range was the 1204, four-berth layout, and this is the one I describe. The 1204 Pioneer was usually based on the CF280 chassis, but I am aware of several that were fitted to the CF350 base, possibly due to a bulk order from a dealer or hire company. This model had a split (stable-type) entrance door (unglazed) on the side of the vehicle, just behind the passenger door. On entering the living area a washroom/shower was positioned immediately on the right-hand side. This contained a tip-up wash basin, vanity unit, shower and electric strip light. The interior walls of this cubicle were lined with a washable vinyl, with a shower tray fitted to the base. Directly opposite the entrance door one faced the wardrobe unit, a three-quarter-height cupboard fitted with shelf and clothes hanging rail. A gas fire of slimline construction was fitted flush with the base of the wardrobe. To the right of this was the cooker, a three-burner hob in stainless steel with a split-folding worktop, which hinged back against the wall. Above the gas hob, at eye-level, was the oven, housed in its own wooden unit, with an extractor hood fitted to the base of the oven unit. On the side of the wardrobe panel, in this kitchen area, was the Zig unit and appropriate electrical fuses (for charging the leisure battery). Beneath the gas hob was a slide-out worktop where one would normally expect to find a grill, but not the best of designs as the refrigerator was housed below this; access to the refrigerator during meal preparation was hindered somewhat if the slide-out worktop was in use. The combined sink/drainer with hot and cold taps was next to the gas hob, with a large storage cupboard below and cutlery drawer in the centre front. The folding work-

The gas water heater and the eye-level oven/grill are mounted above the sink and the cooker.

The view of the kitchen unit as seen from the rear dinette looking forward; small cutlery drawer to the centre of the unit and worktops closed over the hob and sink. The tall wardrobe unit can be seen to the right of this picture and also part of the two-person dinette just behind the driver's seat.

top over the sink/drainer did hinge to one side (towards the rear) in order to provide a small working area, but this in turn protruded over the seating area slightly – a design trait still used by many converters to this day in order to maximize space. Directly above the sink/drainer was an eye-level storage locker, hinged at the top, and fitted to the base of this was an optional gas grill with fold-down front. A small, rectangular, sliding window was positioned on the wall between the sink and the eye-level locker.

To the rear of the living area was the huge dinette, arranged in a U shape and

fitted with luxurious deep foam bases (with backrests). An island-leg table was placed in the centre of the dining area at meal times, with the table having neatly angled corners in order to aid access to and out of the seats. From the kitchen area onward there were eye-level storage lockers right around the rear dinette, joining up with the side wall of the shower unit cubicle opposite the kitchen, giving copious amounts of room for all the camping equipment, books, cosmetics and so on. A pendant light hung from the ceiling in the centre of the dinette area (for use with mains electricity when on-site), and, in

This is the two-person dinette behind the cab seats with the island-leg table in position; this dinette will transform into a single bed with the cushions and backrests.

In a conventional over-cab area there is room to form a double bed, but its owner Tony wanted a six-berth model, so an additional slide-out section was fitted here, allowing three people to sleep in the over-cab section. With the addition of the rear dinette/double bed and the front dinette/single bed there is a total of six berths.

addition to this, there were spotlights fitted in each of the corners. This dinette would convert at night into one huge double bed or two singles, but in either case it meant that the bed bases were an ideal space area for bedding and pillows. Completing this well-appointed area of the living accommodation was a large vanity mirror fitted to a wall of the shower cubicle (facing the kitchen area, not inside shower unit). The interior of the living area was fitted with an ample supply of electric three-pin sockets for use when connected to mains power on-site.

The area to the front of the Pioneer interior had a cut-away section allowing occupants to move from the cab to the living area and vice versa without hitting their heads. This space was bridged with drop-down boards in order to create a double bed in the over-cab section of the vehicle, and one light was fitted in this area as standard. This double bed was accessed by a supplied wooden ladder. Additional features of this Pioneer included fitted carpets in the living area, curtains to all windows and several electric (12V) strip lights in the living areas.

The Pioneer had a freshwater tank (exterior filler) and a waste tank fitted to the underside of the chassis. Hot water came from the Bowen water heater (accessed by a hatch on the exterior), electrically pumped to both the kitchen sink and the shower unit. There was also an exterior storage locker and a similar one for housing two gas cylinders.

As indicated earlier, the Pioneer was available in a bewildering array of base vehicle and berth (sleeping) options, so I shall clarify how the other Pioneer models differed from the one I described above. It was described earlier how the first six-berth model had an extra dining section for two people just behind each front cab seat. These single seats would form an extra single bed at night by using the seat bases and backrests, thus giving five berths with the addition of the double bed at the rear. To create an extra berth and bring the total to six, a sliding platform/base was used in the over-cab area to provide sleeping accommodation for three. In the 1206 six-berth Pioneer models the size of the rear dinette was reduced in order to give an extra dining area for two at the front end, and the subsequent single bed provided by this.

Returning to Tony Willetts, whom I mentioned at the outset, he took delivery of his brand new Pioneer on 2 August 1979 and two days later was heading to Scotland for a ten-day holiday. Despite enduring pouring rain throughout the trip, Tony says that the new Pioneer remained watertight and very snug. Since that maiden journey the first ever six-berth Pioneer has taken Tony to the Isle of Wight, Cornwall, Wales and a return to Scotland. If you are expecting me to report that his Pioneer now has a couple of hundred thousand miles on the clock I shall have to disappoint you, as by 2009 the vehicle had clocked up just 14,000 miles from new. It annually travels the six miles between Tony's house and the local garage in order to have the MOT test carried out. There can be few Pioneer models of this age still in such an incredible condition; the word 'pampered' springs to mind.

During my research on Pioneer models I came across a most interesting letter, which was published in a monthly motorhome magazine in December 1981. Its author was explaining what excellent service he had received from

The Pioneer has the dining area at the rear end of the interior, seen here with the dining table in position; the dinette also transforms into the main double bed.

BELOW: An early two-berth model of the Pioneer during a road test in 1979.

Pioneer of Hull. He had clearly purchased the first Pioneer ever produced, which had been used for demonstration purposes and road tests. A short time after buying it some problems with parts of the bodywork began to surface, no doubt due to rigorous road tests by journalists and numerous demonstration runs. The dealer who had sold it (Windmill Motorhomes) suggested to the owner that the vehicle might require new outer panels in certain places, and an appointment was duly made for its owner to take it to the Pioneer factory in Hull. The owner explained that, although Pioneer had assured him that the vehicle would be ready for collection in under two days, he had taken this statement with a pinch of salt, assuming that Pioneer would come up with all sorts of reason why they had been unable to complete the work in the allotted time. The owner of the Pioneer left the motorhome at the Hull factory at 8.00 a.m., with several workers already beginning to rip outer panels off the vehicle. Returning to the factory at 11.00 a.m.

The eye-level oven/grill in the early two-berth model, with water heater visible to the right.

BELOW: The Pioneer models were produced in fairly substantial numbers throughout the 1980s and seen here is an example on the later (revised) Bedford CF chassis.

on the following day, the owner fully expected the works foreman to be the bearer of bad news about running into problems or having to wait for delivery of new parts, but no, there was the Pioneer sitting in the factory completely ready to be driven away, with a couple of Pioneer staff giving the vehicle a good polish and clean. Not only had Pioneer replaced the outer skin of the motorhome, as agreed, they had also decided to renew the double-glazed windows at no extra cost. The owner was absolutely delighted with the service provided by Pioneer. I have no idea if that Pioneer, supposedly the first one built, is still in use today, but it would be nice to think so, and it could have been the very vehicle that Tony Willetts was so impressed with at that exhibition in 1979.

19

Supreme (CF)

The Bedford Supreme by Supreme Motorhomes Ltd, of Duke Street, London, based on the CF250 chassis; this was a four-berth model with a side-entry door.

Released during the latter half of the 1970s, the Supreme was a coach-built model from Supreme Motor Homes Ltd, of Duke Street in central London. The Supreme was a traditional, four-berth model featuring the over-cab design and side-entrance door, with an outer skin of sheet aluminium, basically following the traditional coach-built construction methods so popular at that time and used on several models such as the Advantura, the Glendale, the Newlander and the Pioneer. The Supreme model is something of an enigma: several examples remain in use today throughout the country, and yet it did not appear in any of the buyers' guides of the time. The Supreme was based on the CF250 chassis and fitted with the 2.3ltr petrol engine as standard, with the 1998cc diesel unit available as an optional extra. An optional overdrive gearbox was also available on the 2.3ltr models.

Supreme Motorhomes certainly went to a great deal of trouble in order to sell their construction techniques to the motorcaravan buyers of the time, and reproduced here is an interesting passage from their glossy sales brochure:

Accent on engineering is the basis of every Supreme Motor Home. It boasts a body structure made entirely from 'hard alloy' extrusions (aluminium alloy with a proof stress in excess of the yield point of ordinary mild steel) which is why we call it our 'Stel-Al' construction system (aluminium that is as strong a steel). The floor frame is the backbone of it all, with tough cross members anchored together with full length through-runners which reach from the back of the cab to the rear end transverse frame member, thus giving maximum strength potential against impact from side or rear, and thereby affording greater passenger safety.

The sides, front and rear frames are jig-built as separate units and are locked together on the floor frame using Avdelok pressure-fixed bolts and collars, and monometal Tucker pop rivets for maximum strength. All exterior panels, including the roof, are aluminium alloy and rib formed for extra strength. They are pre-painted and give a high gloss rust-proof finish. Edge mouldings and drip rails are anodized aluminium with coloured plastic filler strip. A stable-type entrance door is fitted in the nearside of the body allowing access, etc.

I am not sure whether Supreme Motorhomes were attempting to baffle their potential buyers with science, but it did at least sound very convincing, as to whether that sales blurb actually managed to sell any vehicles we can only wonder. In my experience, motorcaravan buyers are drawn to a particular

The rear/side of the Supreme coach-built model with large picture window to the rear end and stepped-up profile above the cab for the double bed.

The interior of the Bedford Supreme looking toward the front from the rear dinette area, with kitchen to the left and the washroom and wardrobe on the right. The Supreme was a well equipped model with gas water heater, oven, extractor, space heater and refrigerator. The furniture finish was a light wood-effect and a fitted carpet was standard.

This particular Bedford Supreme seems to be on its last journey and has clearly sustained some damage over the years. Because there are so few Supreme models still in use, I can only conclude that they must have been produced in fairly limited numbers.

model first by the external appearance, and secondly by the quality and the layout of the interior.

Turning our attention to the inside of the Supreme model, one would enter by a side-entrance door situated just behind the passenger cab door. Directly ahead of this (behind the driver's seat) was the large washroom facility measuring 3ft × 2ft 6in, with a headroom of 6ft 6in. This cubicle was fitted with a wash basin, chemical toilet and shower, together with a roof ventilator, small window (obscure glass fitted) and tile-effect walls. Alongside the washroom was a full-height wardrobe with hanging rail and shelf, with the external door having a long, rectangular vanity mirror attached. At the base of the wardrobe was a storage drawer and below this a gas convector heater/fire and, next to the wardrobe, was a waist-height storage cupboard with worktop.

Opposite the washroom was the kitchen facility, comprising one large cupboard unit which housed the appliances. At the end of the unit (nearest the entrance door) was the two-burner hob with grill and below this a gas oven with fold-down door. At the base of the oven position was a small storage locker, again with drop-down door. Next to the gas hob was a stainless steel sink/drainer, with a cupboard below the sink section (hinged door) and a refrigerator below the drainer. A worktop completed the kitchen unit. At eye-level (above the drainer) was the gas boiler, which provided hot water to the sink and washroom, and an underfloor water tank of 16gal capacity delivered water to the boiler, sink and washroom by an electric pump. Above the gas hob, again at eye-level, was a small cooker hood/extractor, and below this a window giving adequate light for food preparation.

At the rear of the Supreme model was the dinette comprising two bench-style seats (inward facing) with backrests, with an island-leg table erectable at meal times in the centre gangway. The seat bases provided excellent storage space. Along the back of the vehicle was a large opening window, which provided plenty of light to the dinette area and gave good visibility for viewing when parked up. The rear dinette, of course, could be converted into a double bed at night. The interior living area was carpeted throughout and curtains were fitted to all windows. Two spotlights were fitted, one in each corner of the dinette area, and there were eye-level storage lockers right around the rear of the dinette. All the furniture in the Supreme was oak-grained, vinyl-faced particle board of 12mm thickness, finished with hardwood edge moulding.

At the front of the vehicle interior was a further double bed in the over-cab area with a rectangular window at the front with curtains. This bed was reached by a wooden ladder. Other notable features of the Supreme interior included a couple of roof-mounted, opening skylights and several electric strip lights. An external storage locker was provided for the two small gas cylinders and a fire extinguisher was fitted as standard in the living area.

The price of a standard Bedford Supreme model in 1980 was £8,095.

20 *Canterbury Sunhome* (CF)

The Canterbury Sunhome was certainly something very different in the external styling stakes, and that GRP high top, which also protruded over the edges of the body line, was not to everyone's taste. Internally the high top did have the desired effect because, once inside, it did give one the feeling of standing in a small, coach-built model. The example seen here on the sales brochure dates from 1979.

This was an interesting model released by Canterbury Leisure Products of Basildon during the mid 1970s, a panel-van conversion on the CF van with an over- sized GRP high top. Based on the CF250 van, the Sunhome was a slightly different concept in motorcaravan design in order to gain more internal living space. Canterbury had been one of the first converters to offer a high-top panel-van conversion on the Mk.I Ford Transit in the early 1970s, known as the Canterbury

Plainsman. The Plainsman was fitted with a conventional high top, that is to say, it was simply an extension of the Transit van, giving permanent standing room within the vehicle. The Sunhome model, however, was quite different as it did not follow the vehicle's existing sides and rear, instead it had a slight overhang, giving extra space for storage lockers inside. The front also resembled the front section that one would normally associate with a coach-built example, but on the Sunhome the frontal overhang was only slight, with the flat front being fitted with two small windows. The whole roof section was more akin to those often seen on van conversions in the USA and given the name 'turtle-top'.

The whole design idea of the Sunhome was quite clever insomuch that, once inside the vehicle, it gave the impression that you were inside a small, coach-built model, rather than a high-top panel van. There was little by way of innovative design in the Sunhome, except that the use of the high top had allowed the design team to incorporate a full-height shower room. It was simply the deception of extra space in the vehicle created by the extra wide high top which made the Sunhome so interesting.

Based on a CF panel van with twin opening rear doors, the Sunhome had the dinette area at the rear of the vehicle, with a table placed in the central area when dining. The seat cushions could be arranged either as two inward-facing, bench-style seats or an extra cushion could be added across the rear doors to give a U-shaped lounge seating up to six. The rear dinette would convert quickly into a double bed by using the seat bases and backrests. Narrow (in depth) storage lockers were to be found at eye-level in the dinette area, together with small, tinted, acrylic windows incorporated into the sides of the high top at eye-level on either side of the vehicle. Immediately behind the driver's (cab) seat, and adjoining the dinette was the kitchen facility; this was all contained in a cupboard, which had a wood-effect finish. The unit featured a stainless steel sink/drainer, with a cutlery drawer below the drainer section. Strangely, at this period of British motorcaravan development, some converters were still not fitting a refrigerator as part of the standard package,

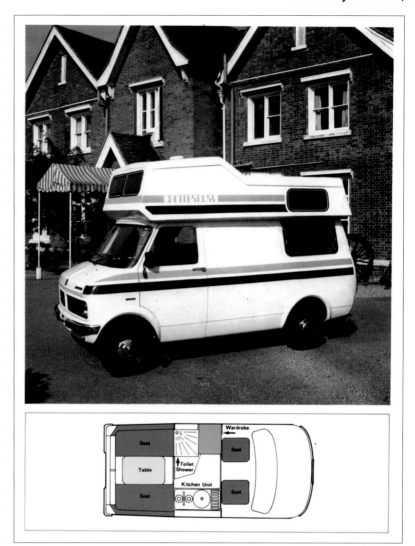

The Sunhome retained the original twin-opening rear doors for entry; there was a dinette at the rear and the washroom/toilet and kitchen unit just behind the cab seats.

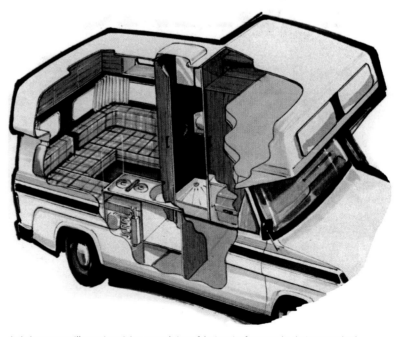

Artist's cut-away illustration giving a good view of the interior features; the design team had managed to fit a shower/washroom into the confines of a panel-van conversion, with the wardrobe alongside housing the chemical toilet in the base. Keen observers will note that the base vehicle shown here is, in fact, a Mk.II Transit, but the interior design was identical to that of the CF.

Original press release photograph of the Canterbury Sunhome interior; the rear dinette has been converted into a double bed and there was a further double situated above the cab. The washroom is to the right and the kitchen on the left (though I have seen them the opposite way around).

and, had one been specified by the customer, this would have been fitted below the sink. The sink/drainer was covered with a matching wood-effect worktop which hinged back against the side of the vehicle when access to the sink was required. A single mixer tap was fitted to the rear of the sink, and this tap would fold down (into the sink) when the worktop was closed. Alongside the sink/drainer was a two-burner gas hob with grill beneath; this had storage cupboards below, not an oven. Once again, a worktop completed the cooker unit, which was hinged back when the cooker was in use; the back was covered with metal in order to protect the underside of the worktop from the flames. At eye-level above the kitchen was a wooden locker, one half of which housed the gas water boiler/heater while the other was fitted with a lift-up door. This was the crockery cupboard and contained shelves for cups, saucers and drinking glasses. On a wide wooden board running along the base of this eye-level unit was an electric strip light. An opening, acrylic, tinted window was positioned just above the sink/drainer unit in order

to allow cooking odours to escape and natural light to come in when cooking was in progress.

Opposite the kitchen facilities was the washroom equipped with shower, tip-up wash basin, vanity unit and light. The whole interior was lined with a patterned waterproof vinyl. Water for the shower and basin was heated by the gas boiler above the kitchen unit and delivered by an electric pump from the underfloor water container (filled through a nozzle within the engine compartment). Alongside the washroom was a full-height wardrobe unit fitted with hanging rail and shelves; incorporated into the top of the wardrobe was a bedside storage unit for use by the occupants of the over-cab bed. At the base of the wardrobe was provision for the storage of a chemical toilet (for when the shower was being used).

At the front of the Sunhome, in the over-cab area, was a double bed measuring 5ft 10in × 3ft 7in, with a wooden access ladder provided. The front section of the roof in this bed area had two small windows (non-opening) fitted with curtains, and an electric light. Centrally

located in the roof was a ventilator, with a further and larger ventilator also in a central position in the main living area. Curtains were fitted to all the windows of the living area as standard, with vinyl cushion flooring in the kitchen area and fitted carpet in the dinette. All of the Sunhome interior was double insulated throughout, including the GRP roof. The Canterbury Sunhome was available in one colour scheme – an off-white exterior with contrasting brown and yellow bands both around the roof and the vehicle waistband; the name 'Canterbury' was visible on either side of the frontal roof section.

The Sunhome was available on both the Bedford CF and the Mk.II Ford Transit, and in terms of the surviving models, I have to say that they are extremely rare with only a limited number still in use. As a guide price, the Sunhome (in standard form) was £5,803 in April 1979. There were two other panel-van conversions from the same period, which utilized a similar but not identical roof style: these were the Holdsworth Hi-Flyer (Mk.I and Mk.II Transit) and the Bedford Invincible (CF), all of which are now very rare indeed.

assorted CF-based camper vans

Custom 'street' or 'day' vans were much in vogue during the 1970s and the 1980s, and the Bedford CF was a perfect candidate for DIY conversion; one company spotted this opening in the marketplace and released a range of camper vans with a custom influence. Seen here is one of their models, the Stratus 250 High Top; other models in the range included the Stratus 250 (factory roof), the Cumulus 280 (tin top) and the Cirrus 280-7 (tin top).

THE BACKGROUND

When one takes a look at the full list of camper vans that were built on the CF chassis between 1969 and 1987 and then considers the number of examples of the most popular models produced during that period, it is not difficult to see why so many have survived to this day and are still in regular use. Sadly, the largest producers of these models from the 1970s and the 1980s are no longer trading, both Dormobile and CI Autohomes closed down during the 1990s and all production records were destroyed. Similarly, converters such as Holdsworth, Glendale, Advantura, Supreme, Pioneer, Canterbury and others have been consigned to history.

In my descriptive chapters about Bedford camper vans I have tried to feature the best-selling models based on the CF chassis during its long production run. Obviously these chapters only scratch the surface since there were quite literally dozens of different campers and motorhomes, and so this chapter will offer an insight into some of the less well known conversions,

models with limited runs and some that simply failed to sell in significant numbers. It would be fair to say that the majority of these early models sold reasonably well, a new chassis often attracts a sudden influx of buyers, and this was the case with those early examples by Dormobile, namely the Romany II and the Debonair II.

This trend continued during the early 1970s, and the Freeway, again by Dormobile, became one of the best selling models of the period. The Bedouin Mk.I, Brigand and the Olsen-designed Autohome captured a large slice of the motorcaravan market for CI Autohomes. Auto-Sleepers had gained a reputation for quality interiors with their Commer model and they transferred this layout over to the CF chassis with great sales success. But sandwiched in between all the popular CF campers being produced by the major converters were others being converted by much smaller companies, offering limited production runs. Some of these companies did specialize in motorcaravan production, while others, such as trailer caravan manufacturers and boat builders, saw it as an

opportunity to diversify their business interests. Obviously within a single chapter I cannot mention every single CF-based camper van and motorhome, but I endeavour to touch upon some of these lesser known models produced over the years.

CAVALIER COACHMAN

Cavalier Coachman of Felixstowe, Suffolk produced some very futuristic-looking campers based on the Bedford CF, which were much in vogue during the late 1970s and the early 1980s when the British 'custom' scene was in full swing. Many van owners during this time were carrying out the full customization, which included some very abstract paint schemes, the fitting of non-standard shaped windows, adding bigger chrome wheels and fat tyres and then fitting out the interiors to their own tastes. The Cavalier Coachman company saw a gap in the camper van market for a production 'street van', and came up with several models based on the CF, which reflected the whole custom scene. These were the Stratus 250,

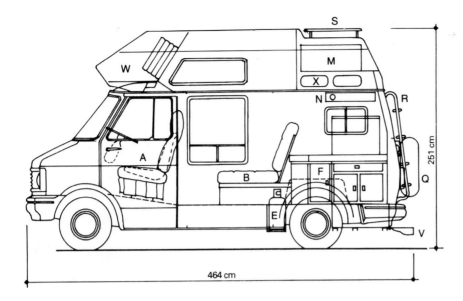

Key

A – Recl./Swivel Chair
B – Passenger Seat
C – Single Fold Bed
D – Removable Table
E – Gas Bottle (6kg)
F – Kitchen Unit
G – Refrigerator
H – Storage Cupboard
J – Wardrobe (180cm)
K – Toilet Area
L – Standing Well (250cm)
M – Kitchen Locker
N – Extractor Fan
O – Kitchen Window
P – Bay Window
Q – Wheel Carrier
R – Ladder
S – Roof Rack
T – Radio Aerial (option)
V – Drop Step (option)
W – Front Locker with
      Fold Up Bed
      and Mattresses
X – Top Locker

ABOVE: Side view and floor plan of the Stratus 250 High Top model.

The Stratus 250 (non-high top model) on display at a sales stand during a Thames Valley motorhome show during the 1980s. The colour scheme was brown and gold with bold bodywork graphics; note the deep side-tinted window and raised roof section to the rear.

effect, both inside and outside their vehicles. They were most striking, though I cannot say whether they were a huge sales success. But, having been around motorcaravans for around forty years, I can honestly say that I have only ever seen a few Cavalier vans in the flesh. They were quite rare even when new, leaving them few and far between today. Their prices, as of spring 1981, were as follows:

- Stratus 250, £4,070
- Stratus high top, £3,826
- Cumulus, £4,637
- Cirrus, £3,617.

The option of a high-top Cumulus was given in 1981 at £5,112. The list of optional extras was quite bewildering; some examples are:

- digital quartz clock with double aircraft lights, £90

the Stratus 250 high top, the Cumulus 280 and the Cirrus 280-7, with the Bedford CF Roadcruiser later added to the range. With the exception of the Stratus 250 high top, none of these models had a rising roof fitted but retained the original factory metal roof.

The fashionable colours of the time included brown, orange, gold and yellow, and Cavalier used these to good

- driver's cup tray and dashboard furnishing, £56
- convector floor heater, £272
- roof-mounted air conditioner, £451
- 12V shaver point, £32
- roller blinds, £34 (each)

- roof vent, £147
- mini sun roof, £63
- de luxe Tygan bunk beds (Cumulus), £143
- complete set of front spoilers and wheel flairs, £194.

INCA

One company that gained a very good reputation for their conversions during the 1970s was Cooper & Griffin (later Cooper Motor Caravans) of Rugby,

RIGHT: *The Inca model on the CF chassis, a panel-van conversion by Cooper Motor Caravans Ltd, of Rugby, Warwickshire, and fitted with the Sherwood solid-sided roof: this particular example dates from 1972.*

Cut-away illustration of the Inca, which features a forward position dinette/double bed, cooker and sink opposite each other and wardrobe to the corner. Two children's bunks were provided, one each in the roof section and the cab.

This stunning example is the customized CF Inca once owned by Terry and Maureen Acreman. This camper van was given a beautiful paint finish, fitted with non-standard wheels, front-lower spoiler and some pretty impressive front lights. The Inca was the winner of several trophies during Terry's ownership, and a couple of those can be seen here.

Warwickshire. Their Inca model on the CF was a panel-van conversion with rising roof and featured a traditional layout with the dinette/double bed just behind the cab seats. Furniture was arranged toward the rear with the kitchen to one side and a storage unit and wardrobe opposite. Both the internal layout and the style were similar to those of another Midlands-based converter named Car-Campers, and I have known some owners of these models to be confused as to which one they had actually bought (on the Mk.I Transit at least, as Car-Campers did not convert the CF). The Inca made use of the solid-sided Sherwood rising roof, which did blend well with the lines of the CF in the closed position. As an example of price, a four-berth model on the CF 18cwt chassis would have cost around £1,677 in 1973. Optional extras included:

- chemical toilet, £31
- fire/heater, £11.50
- steering lock, £6.70
- refrigerator, £35
- radio/tape player, £79.

MURVI

Built by Nomadic Wheels Ltd of Totnes, Devon the Murvi range of camper vans has been in production for many years. Murvi quickly built up a reputation as being extremely versatile vehicles, almost using the early Dormobile strategy of complete versatility – estate car to caravan. Murvi models were always aimed at the buyers who wanted something just that little bit different, an everyday vehicle that would quickly convert into a mobile office and/or a camper. This is best summed up by a quotation from their sales literature of the early 1980s:

> astonishingly versatile – within a couple of minutes it changes from an estate car seating up to nine, to a 2+2 berth camper, to a car with a boot, to a load carrier. And it's all done with ease and style.

I think that description paints a perfect picture of what a Murvi was/is.

Taking 1985 as an example, there were five models in the Murvi range based on the Bedford CF, these were:

- Murvi Mondo C, £9,820
- Murvi Executive Custom, £10,717
- Murvi Mondo S, £11,305
- Murvi Mondo S+, £13,087
- Murvi Executive Super, £15,888.

The base vehicle used by Murvi for these models was the CF250 van with the 2ltr petrol engine, a diesel engine was optional (an extra £850) on all the models. The Murvi was certainly an attractive vehicle, with two-tone metallic paintwork and colour-coded grille and bumpers (fenders). The colour options were silver, gold, blue and green. In order to give some idea of the standard fittings in a Murvi I shall take the Murvi Mondo S+ model: wide rear doors, hinged side door with bottle cabinet and small table, cruise control, Panasonic radio/cassette, multi-option rear seat, an estate car, sitting room, office or camper layout (all obtainable in just 2min), an additional child's bunk, freshwater storage, wash basin, galley kitchen with hob/grill, table and storage, wardrobe, blown-air heating, glass sunroofs, front-tinted windows and four electric strip lights.

The Murvi range of van conversions have been around for a number of years and must lay claim to being one of the first true MPV models, a true utility vehicle capable of being used as an everyday car for passenger transport, an estate/load carrier, mobile office and a camper van. A Bedford CF example is seen here, though the Murvi vans have been produced on a wide variety of chassis over the years from their Devon base.

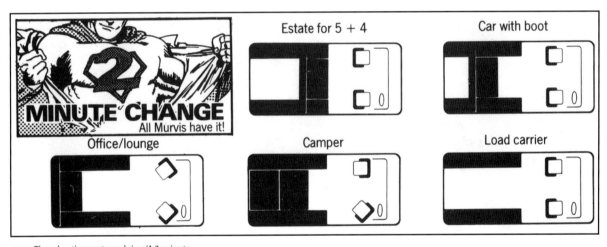

ABOVE: *The advertisement proclaims 'A 2-minute change–all Murvis have it', a slogan emphasizing the fact that the vehicle can be changed from one mode to another in just 2min.*

RIGHT: *Press picture dating from 1979 with an early Murvi interior on display; the central cabinet housed a myriad of features, a bit like a magic box. Furniture at that time was made of real wood, later changed in favour of wipe-clean laminate units. Note the low roofline in the interior as the majority of Murvi conversions (of that period) did not have a rising roof or high top fitted.*

assorted CF-based camper vans

SUNTREKKER

Once a popular motorcaravan concept, especially during the 1970s and 1980s, the dismountable (or demountable) unit was, and still is, a far more common sight in the USA than in Britain. Although only a limited number of dismountable models were available here, by far the best selling example of these was the Suntrekker by B. Walker & Son Ltd, of Watford, Hertfordshire. This type of unit

could be dismounted from the bed of the vehicle by the use of metal legs, thus allowing the vehicle to be driven away and leave the living unit on site. It also gave the owner the advantage of being able to store the unit when it was not required, yet still leave the vehicle free to be used for other purposes.

Suntrekker units were built specifically for certain vehicles, thus there was one built each just for the Land Rover, the Morris Marina, the Mazda one-ton pick-

up and the Volkswagen LT. The 'universal' Suntrekker unit was designed to fit the following chassis: the Ford Transit, the Leyland Sherpa, the Mercedes L306D, the Toyota Hi-ace and the Bedford CF. This universal unit as fitted to the CF had an overall length of 13ft 3in, a width of 6ft 3in and an overall height of 6ft 9in. With an easy-lift jacking system, the Suntrekker unit could be removed from the vehicle in a matter of minutes. The unit itself was constructed by using a fibre-

ABOVE: Demountable living units have never really been as popular in Britain as they are in many other countries, most notable the USA. A leading constructor of such models in this country was Walker with their Suntrekker examples, a mid 1970s model CF is seen here.
LEFT: The Suntrekker units were available for a wide variety of base vehicles and were designed to be demounted from their donor chassis when on site by using the support legs, one of which can be seen here.

glass roof and aluminium sides; it had a single rear-door entry and was fitted with a roof ventilator. Interior features included an over-cab double bed, dining area/double bed, kitchen with stainless steel sink, two-burner hob and grill, two freshwater containers, washroom/shower and toilet, ample storage lockers/units, electric lighting and provision for two gas cylinders.

Although I have described the complete universal system as fitted to the CF and other chassis, it was possible to order a plain Suntrekker shell devoid of interior fittings. The purchaser then had the opportunity to buy as much or as little from the Suntrekker list as he wished. In 1976 the universal shell only (no interior) carried a price of £966 including VAT, the easy-jacking system was a further £205, furniture/cupboards were £225, sink and cooker £64 and, finally, soft furnishings were £135. There was a vast array of optional extras, which included: a modified six-berth layout, water heater, double glazing, flyscreens, intercom system, folding double step and a second battery system.

In addition to the Suntrekker dismountable there were several other converters building these units to fit the Bedford CF, some of which were the Challenger by Motor Bodies of Bideford, Devon, the Multicruiser by Multicruiser Ltd of Bradford and the Westcraft by Westcraft Motorhomes, also of Bideford. To see any of these dismountable units today, still mounted on their original chassis, is extremely rare. Many surviving units will by now have been fitted to much later chassis.

WORCESTER

I include the very large Worcester coachbuilt model here for two reasons, one being slightly selfish on my part, and the other to highlight the sheer size and cost of the Worcester back in 1982. With regard to the first, I was brought up in the city of Worcester and well remember this motorcaravan dealership, which was situated just outside the city in the village of Fernhill Heath. The Bedford CF Worcester is one of the few associations that the city has ever had with motorcaravanning

in general, but one has to say that it was a very impressive motorhome. Which leads me to my second reason, it was one of the biggest and most expensive British models at the time, costing a staggering £19,000 (I bought a two-bedroom house in Worcester in that same year for £15,500). In fairness, I should point out that it was just about the most comprehensively equipped motorhome manufactured in the country up to that point.

The Worcester was based on the CF350 LWB twin rear-wheeled chassis and was fitted with the 2.3ltr petrol engine as standard, with a 2.3ltr diesel available at extra cost. This model was launched to rival the large American motorhomes that were gaining in popularity in Britain in the early 1980s. The Worcester CF would certainly never win any prizes for beauty; it was, in effect, a huge, long box with little in the way of contours and a complete lack of smooth GRP panels. It was only recently that I discovered that KJ Caravans (makers of the Glendale) had built the original prototype, a fact which appears

The luxurious Worcester motorhome on the CF was a one-off release from Richard Smith & Father, a motorhome sales company based just outside Worcester. It was aimed at being a cross between a large British motorhome and an American RV, and at that the time it was. By today's standards, it would be considered a relatively medium-sized model, but back then you could actually buy a decent house for the same price as this model.

THE WORCESTER

BRITISH
AND PROUD OF IT

We have taken the **BEST** features and spec
from British and American Motor Homes
and designed them **BETTER** for you
it's all in the new **WORCESTER**
Right-Hand Drive Bedford based Coach built Motor Home

The Ultimate in Luxury and Value from Hereford & Worcester Premier
Motor Caravan Centre

RICHARD SMITH & FATHER
(THE FAMILY BUSINESS BUILT ON TRUST, CONFIDENCE AND SATISFACTION)
MAIN ROAD GARAGE ★ FERNHILL HEATH ★ WORCESTER
Tel: 0905 53290 (24 hours)
Designed by Maslen Shutler Associates. Built by K. J. Caravans, Hull
OUR OPENING HOURS ARE:
Monday to Friday 8.30am—6.30pm ★ Saturday 9am—5pm ★ Sunday 2pm—5pm
or other hours by arrangement

obvious when you study pictures of the Worcester and the Glendale side by side. But it would appear that KJ Caravans had gone into liquidation soon after building the prototype and so the production models of the Worcester were built by Bedford Coachworks of Wilstead (builders of Cotswold Motorcaravans in the 1970s) for Richard Smith & Father of Fernhill Heath, Worcester.

There would be little point in my giving a full description of the Worcester interior because it was made perfectly clear in several road test reports of the time that, after the prototype had appeared, buyers would be allowed to choose their own interior style and layout. The prototype had a single entry door at the rear, but plans were afoot to build side-entrance models also, and, in addition, customers would have the option of a rear lounge, as opposed to the front lounge in the prototype. But whatever layout was chosen, the high level of standard specifications would remain the same, and these included: Woolfrace high back seats in the cab, spacious lounge, full toilet/shower room, hot and cold running water, water heater, room heater, on-board generator, external storage lockers, roof rack and access ladder, large over-cab double bed, full gas cooker, pantry, full wardrobe, refrigerator, television and video recorder, eye-level storage lockers throughout, fully carpeted floor, tinted sliding windows and mains electric hook-up.

ABOVE: Period advertisement for the Worcester motorhome, which proclaims that it was actually built by KJ Caravans, who also produced the Glendale range.

RIGHT: Not given its own chapter here, but certainly worth mentioning was the Deauville coach-built model by Dormobile, an award-winning model based on the CF, which was one of the last great models built at Folkestone.

A road test reporter for *Motorcara-van + Motorhome Monthly* said this of the Worcester model in 1982:

I liked the body style, standard of finish inside and out, the Bedford's perform-ance, carpet in the cab, captain's seats, the large bathroom, plenty of kitchen work space, the firm, large table and the pull-out pantry. I would have liked a wider entrance, better rear view mir-rors, electric light in the over-cab bed, a wider over-cab bed, exterior hardware locker and a bigger wardrobe. I did not like-the slow draining sink.

I have no doubt that these minor niggles were sorted out on future models because the majority of converters did take note of road test reports in such publications.

ABOVE: *The Bedford CF chassis was used for conversion to a passenger-carrying bus during its long production run, and when these vehicles finished their fare-paying service they made an excellent base for home-converted motorhomes; one such example is seen here.*

LEFT: *Ambulance conversions to motorhomes have been around for a long time; there are a large number of Bedford CF examples still in use around Britain.*

Following on from Bedford bus and ambulance conversions, the ex-Bedford coaches are always in demand as a base for large DIY motorhomes as they offer great scope.

22

Bedford Midi *camper vans*

The Midihome by Autohomes of Poole, a high-top camper van conversion on the Bedford Midi, advertised as their 'silver dream machine'. Launched in the late summer of 1985, the Midihome, like similar conversions on the Bedford Midi, enjoyed only moderate sales success, despite being a well designed model.

The 1-ton Bedford Midi van was launched in 1984, with a long and sleek design, it had a styling reminiscent of the Japanese light commercials of the time. It quickly became a popular van with tradesmen but it was less well received by the motorcaravan converters. In order to become a camper van, the Midi would require an internal design layout that placed all the furniture down one side and utilized a rear double seat that could transform into a double bed. That layout was well established in the Volkswagen T2 and T3 vans, as well as the Toyota Hi-Ace, light commercial vehicles that had been tried and tested over many years. The Midi was a newcomer and yet it would be competing with the iconic VW for sales, but it never therefore really stood

any chance of success as a camper-van base. The Midi was, in effect, a Luton-built Isuzu van, and, in retrospect, it did deserve to make a much bigger impact upon the British motorcaravan scene than it actually did.

The original engine options were a 1.8ltr petrol or 2ltr diesel, later expanding to 2ltr petrol, 2.2ltr diesel and 2.4ltr turbo diesel units. In standard form, the Midi was supplied with a floor-mounted gear change (five-speed), but a column change option was available allowing a third (central) cab seat to be fitted. The Midi was available in two lengths, a short wheelbase (14.7ft) and a long wheelbase (15.9ft). It was available with single or twin side sliding doors, single-piece tailgate, standard factory metal roof or semi-high top. A £10 million investment

had been made at the Luton plant on anti-corrosion techniques and a further £25 million spent on a new paint section, and, as a result, the Midi came with a six-years' manufacturer's warranty.

The option of a chassis-cowl did not exist, so converters were unable to fit a coach-built motorhome to the Midi. As it happened, the converters were even reluctant to transform the basic van into a camper conversion. Only three British converters of note decided to offer camper models on the Midi, these were Autohomes, Auto-Sleepers and Devon, and, as one would expect from three of the country's leading motorcaravan specialists, each produced a fine, Midi-based camper conversion. Those three firms produced the Midihome (Autohomes), the Auto-Sleeper Midi and two choices from Devon – the Dove and the Domino. With the exception of the Devon Dove (rising roof), they were all high-top models, and all four had the single-piece tailgate and one side, sliding door.

AUTOHOMES MIDIHOME

The Midihome by Autohomes of Poole, Dorset was launched during a huge open weekend at the south-coast factory in 1985. Based on the LWB Midi chassis with a single side-entry door (sliding) and one-piece rear tailgate, the Midihome was fitted with a stylish high top giving full standing height over two-thirds of the interior with a lowered front section. It was launched as the Silver Dream Machine, with the first fifty models being given a silver metallic paint finish. One thing that was synonymous with Autohomes designs of that period was the well-planned interior layouts. Because of the long, thin space in the Midi it would have been quite simple just to fit a Volkswagen-style interior, but the Autohomes design team gave much more thought than that to the internal space and came up with something quite innovative. They designed the 'three room concept', consisting of three distinct areas: driving cab, kitchen and living area. The driving cab is self-explanatory, but they created a large, U-shape lounge in the centre of the vehicle, in line with the sliding side door, which converted into a double bedroom at night. The rear of the living space was dedicated to the kitchen and was well equipped; it included an enamelled hob with grill and a toughened glass cover, matching sink/drainer with a chopping board, refrigerator,

water heater and numerous storage cupboards and drawers. The rear section of the high-top roof was thoughtfully fitted with small, tinted windows, which allowed plenty of light to filter through, but, in addition, there were large windows fitted to the rear side bodywork in the kitchen area, and, of course, the top half of the rear tailgate section. Electric strip lights were fitted at eye-level and curtains were supplied for all windows. This kitchen area had the added benefit of being a dual-purpose room as a full-height wardrobe door could be opened and used to screen off the kitchen from the lounge, thus creating a private washroom/toilet/changing facility.

Other features of the Midihome included mains electric hook-up, built-in 18gal water tank (with water-level gauge), waste-water tank and double-skinned, fully insulated vehicle bodywork. Curtains were fitted to all windows, the flooring consisted of vinyl in the rear kitchen and carpet in the lounge, there were several electric strip lights throughout the interior and wood-grain finish to all the furniture. Optional extras included: electrical control panel/second (leisure) battery, flush chemical toilet, child's bed and a blown-air heating system. The Autohomes Midihome had a list price of £11,299 in February 1986 (two-berth, with the option of a third).

AUTO-SLEEPER MIDI

One of the most respected names in Britain for motorcaravan conversions, Auto-Sleepers, unveiled their Midi model at Earls Court in 1985. It was based on the LWB Midi and fitted with the 1.8ltr

petrol engine as standard, with a diesel at extra cost. The Auto-Sleeper Midi was certainly an attractive camper, fitted with their own high top (William Towns design) and with bold exterior coach-line graphics around both the roof and the camper, it was a real head turner. The interior was of typical Auto-Sleeper quality, though there was little by way of innovation about the layout, Auto-Sleepers using the tried and trusted formula found in their Volkswagen VT20 (rising roof) and VHT (high top) of the time. There was certainly nothing wrong with this, as their Volkswagen VHT model won the title of 'Motor Caravan of the Year' in 1985.

The furniture in the Auto-Sleeper Midi was set out along one side and behind the driver's seat; and running front to back it consisted of a vitreous enamel sink/drainer, cooker and three-way refrigerator. These appliances were housed in superb Auto-Sleeper cabinet work of wood-grain faces with a hard-wood edging, all built to exacting standards. These cupboards had copious amounts of storage space, cutlery drawer and worktops; there was provision in the base of one cupboard to house a chemical toilet. Alongside the kitchen appliances was a slimline storage cupboard (top hinged), which was deep enough to carry the provisions for several days. In the rear (at the far end of all these units) was the wardrobe with side-hinged door, this contained a shelf and clothes rail. To the rear, just behind the double bench seat, was a large luggage area, ideal for storing camping accessories and this was finished with a parcel shelf (removable). The double seat ran three-quarters width across the interior and was

Day

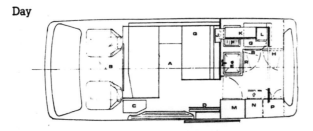

Night

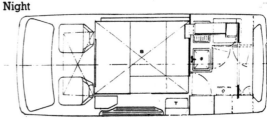

A. Dinette Seats	F. Drainer	L. Water Heater	R. Storage Cupboards
B. Overcab storage	G. Hob & Grill Unit	M. Wardrobe	S. Double Bed
C. Battery Access	H. Refrigerator	N. Waste Bin	T. Hinged Table
D. Table Storage	J. Electrics	P. Gas Bottle Storage	
E. Sink	K. Eye Level Shelf	Q. Fresh Water Tank	

A detailed floor plan of the Autohomes Midihome, which featured a U-shaped lounge/dinette and a rear L-shaped kitchen, capable of being closed off from the lounge to provide a private washing/changing area.

ABOVE: This is the Auto-Sleeper conversion of the Bedford Midi, a very appealing model with a well crafted high top; distinctive side graphics enhance the fluid lines of the Midi exterior. Due to the long, thin shape of the Midi, it was crying out for a Volkswagen-style interior, and this is exactly what Auto-Sleepers fitted – hand-crafted units all along one side, pull-down rear seat/ double bed and side-door access. I am reliably informed that fewer than fifty examples were built in 1985–86, which would account for the fact that I have been unable to track one down to inspect.

LEFT: Earls Court, November 1985 and the new Auto-Sleeper Midi is put on public view.

hinged so that the base and backrest formed a double bed. There was yet further storage space below the seat base. An island-leg table completed the lounge area when dining. The Auto-Sleeper Midi was a four-berth model, with two housed in the high top roof.

According to company records, fewer than fifty of these models were ever produced. The list price of the Auto-Sleeper Midi in January 1986 was £11,574. There are some surviving examples, though by this time it is likely that they have been resprayed, possibly in a custom colour, and the trademark auto-sleeper graphics deleted.

DEVON

Devon conversions produced two models based on the Midi: a rising roof example, model name Dove, and a high-top version, Domino. Both models were based on the LWB Midi and fitted with the 1.8ltr petrol engine as standard, with a diesel unit at extra cost. The Dove version featured the Devon Double Top rising roof, side-hinged and operated via two gas struts. This roof could accommodate two adults in the large bed. The two internal layouts were very similar; both had a sliding side door and one-piece tailgate.

Devon did not opt for a traditional Volkswagen layout, but, instead, placed the kitchen facilities to the rear end. The kitchen was well equipped with gas hob, oven and grill, sink/drainer and ample storage lockers, floor-mounted and at eye-level. Seating in the Devon Midi was situated midway along the internal space, in line with the side door. The seats (both doubles) were housed on box bases with supported backrests and, in the Dove model, could be placed in the forward-facing position (omnibus style) for travelling. For dining the seats were placed to face one another, with an island-leg table in

ABOVE: Devon Conversions decided to convert the Midi in 1986 and came up with two models. The Dove, seen here on the left, was fitted with the Devon 'Double Top' rising roof, a four-berth model, which included a refrigerator as part of the standard equipment; and the Devon Domino, a high-top model, which was comprehensively equipped as standard.

RIGHT: Devon Conversions are thought of as the Volkswagen camper van specialist, and they have produced some beautiful VW models over the years; seen here as part of their 1986 line-up is the Bedford Midi Dove and the Domino sandwiched between a VW Eurovette and a VW Caravette.

the middle. The seat bases also provided good storage space. In the high-top Domino the seats for the lounge were situated in an L shape, and a portable table (with four legs) was provided for dining.

I have not been able to trace a single surviving Devon Midi, so I shall have to rely on the testimony of a road-test reporter of the time who stated that both models were finished to a high standard, but added that the kitchen area in the rear of the Domino appeared slightly more cramped than that in the Dove. This may possibly have had something to do with the high-top roof's not extending right to the far end of the rear, thus restricting the headroom for slightly taller occupants. The high-top Domino had the additional feature of a storage locker built into the front area (this also housed the dining table) above the cab. Both models were fully insulated and fitted with curtains to all windows. The interior of both models featured cabinet work in a wood-grain effect finish with light (solid) wood edging to cupboard doors. Mains electric hook-up was fitted in both models as part of the standard equipment package.

The list price for the Devon Dove in 1986 was £11,513 and £11,712 for the Domino.

The little Danbury Renegade based on the 970cc Bedford Rascal must have been one of the smallest camper vans ever produced in any volume. With an overall length of 10ft 9.3in and an overall height of 7ft 5in with the roof raised it really was a very compact camper. The Danbury advertising of the time for the Renegade summed up this model perfectly:

'The Motor caravan built to be used for 52 weeks of the year' – don't buy a camper to be used for a few weeks of the year, buy a Danbury and get real value for your money. Danbury have taken this little van and turned it into a practical motor caravan with room to stand, sleep, cook and eat, without detracting from the vehicle's excellent road performance and economy. A full length, fibreglass elevating roof has been fitted to ensure plenty of headroom when parked for camping – and yet, when the roof is safely anchored down for driving, the overall height is still only 6ft 4in. So your Danbury Camper is capable of being parked in the average domestic garage, and taken shopping to the local multi-storey car park.

The family behind the Danbury name were the Dawsons, who had been producing some excellent camper conversions for years before releasing the Danbury Renegade, and were based in Needham Market, Suffolk. Essentially the Renegade model was a two-person camper and was based on the Rascal van with sliding side doors (both sides of the van) and one-piece tailgate. Directly behind the two cab seats was a box-style bench seat, with two separate foam backrests, and designed to seat two people facing rearward. But this was no ordinary bench seat since concealed beneath it was a stainless steel sink (with tap) and a two-burner hob with grill, these two kitchen appliances being raised from within the bench seat once the padded seat base was hinged backward. To the rear of the interior was a further (upholstered) bench seat with backrests, and an island-leg table was placed in the centre of the living area floor when dining. There was storage space beneath the rear seat and further luggage space to the rear of the seat, with a wardrobe

23

Danbury Renegade (Rascal)

The little Renegade by Danbury based on the Bedford Rascal was a small, compact camper van with one double bed, a small rising roof, basic cooker and sink and a wardrobe.

The cooker and sink in the Renegade are housed in the seat base, just behind the cab seats; the cooker can be seen in the foreground with the sink at the far end.

positioned to one side, with a fitted clothes rail.

At night both the forward seat and the rear seat were used to form a double bed, which stretched from behind the cab seats to the very rear of the vehicle. Given that the sleeping arrangements accounted for the whole of the available floor space, I suspect that anyone purchasing a Renegade would have found it a requirement to have an awning attached to either the side or the rear of the vehicle in which to store a chemical toilet. Danbury stated in their sales literature that there was

provision under the rear seat to store a small chemical toilet, but one would assume that this was for travelling purposes only, as using it once the double bed had been assembled would have been nigh on impossible. All the furniture in the Renegade was made from real wood with an attractive oak veneer finish, with a final lacquer to protect the veneer from knocks. An electric light was provided for the living area and curtains were fitted to all windows as part of the standard finish. Water was pumped to the small sink from a water carrier (supplied). The delightful rising

The view through the side door with both front and rear bench-style seats visible.

All the cushions from the seats are brought into play here to form the double bed, which covers much of the space in the Renegade.

roof, featuring coloured stripes on the canvas, was of the full-length variety, covering the whole of the interior roof space.

The Renegade was an ideal 'weekender' vehicle, and a camper well suited for picnics and days out; and, of course, it was perfect as an everyday utility vehicle. The Danbury Renegade had a list price of £8,436 (including taxes) in 1987. Optional extras included cab seats upholstered to match those in the rear at £50 each, and the fitting of a single bunk bed in the rising roof at £75. In addition to the Renegade, Danbury also produced the Danbury Fun Camper model, again based on the Rascal van, but this model was not fitted with a rising roof. It did have a cooker, sink and twin beds and carried a price tag of £7,470. The option of having a Danbury rising roof fitted to the Fun Camper was charged at £750.

ABOVE: The Renegade was a well planned camper van; seen here is the rear of the vehicle interior with the tailgate raised.

BELOW LEFT: An alternative side view of the Danbury Renegade with the roof raised; the passenger side had an extra window fitted.

BELOW RIGHT: Despite its diminutive size, the Danbury Renegade had no shortage of entry/exit points, as this pictures verifies; two cab doors, two side doors and a rear tailgate.

24

Autohomes Bambi (Rascal)

ABOVE: This was the scene in the holding park at the Autohomes factory in the mid 1980s, a line-up of Bambis waiting to be born.

LEFT: The Bedford-based Bambi motorhome by Autohomes of Poole really is a cracking little vehicle, an ideal touring base for a couple and well equipped for such a small model. The Bambi has an enthusiastic following, with an active owners club, and, with plenty of good examples still around, they tend to hold good prices in the used camper market.

The Autohomes Bambi model based on the Bedford Rascal has to be one of the most extraordinary little camper vans ever produced, within Britain, at least. It was a huge sales success for Dorset-based Autohomes, which had begun life as Caravan International (Motorised) Ltd in the 1960s (and Blue-bird before then). They had a knack of delivering some innovative interior designs and layouts, and the Bambi was the culmination of many years' experience gained in the motorcaravan market. As was often the case in previous years, motor manufacturers would invite motorcaravan converters to view

any new light commercial chassis before any official press launches, and this was the case with the Bedford Rascal built at Luton. On seeing the tiny Rascal van for the first time, the Autohomes chairman, Ian Macpherson, decided that the small confines of the basic delivery van would not offer sufficient internal space in which to create a fully fledged camper. However, also on display on that day was a pick-up version of the Rascal and no doubt Ian's mind went into overdrive about the possibilities that the little pick-up suggested.

By the early summer of 1986 Autohomes had made a prototype coach-

built camper using the Rascal pick-up base, and it was unveiled to the press at the Luton Vauxhall/Bedford plant in June of that year. The overwhelming view of those present was complete agreement that the new Bambi would be a success. It was clever in the extreme to make a very small coach-built model on the back of such a little pick-up; it had obviously taken a great deal of planning, and it paid off. That prototype, registration number C665 CEL, was offered for road test to several publications, and, despite some minor dissatisfaction, the majority of the test reports concluded that the Bambi was an excellent, compact camper, well built and well designed. In fact, the Bambi was so well received that orders for the new model placed that June accounted for the entire factory production through to October. But the sales success of the new Bambi did not end there as there was reputed to be a waiting list for a further three years, such was the demand for the coach-built micro-camper.

The body and floor of the Bambi were constructed from vacuum-bonded, styrene sandwich boards, making the body extremely light yet very strong and offering excellent insulation qualities. Entry to the living area was by a single rear door of the 'stable type', in two parts and therefore allowing the top half of the door to be left open in warm weather when the vehicle was parked. Both the top and the bottom of the door were glazed, which meant that the driver had some degree of visibility through the rear view mirror and the bottom door panel when parking. The rear of the living area was a recessed section, lower than the floor area in the rest of the vehicle (due to the overhang of the body beyond the pick-up base) and this lower floor section gave a standing height of 6ft 2in. Within this rear section were the kitchen to the left and the sink/wardrobe to the right. The kitchen consisted of a two-burner hob with grill, and a three-way refrigerator built in below; a copper-effect splash panel was fitted around the rear corner of the interior side walls, offering protection when cooking. Above the gas hob was a storage

A refurbished Bambi with over-cab window, front bull-bar and the addition of a side pull-out sun awning; few remaining models still in use will now be in a completely 'as new' form, most have had some modifications and enhancements.

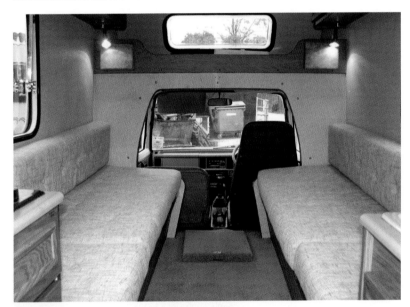

This is the beautifully restored interior of the same model.

View of the rear corner; seen here is the sink with a storage cupboard below, to the side is the hinged worktop and to the rear, above the sink, is the wardrobe, storage space inside of which is dropped down behind the sink.

The opposite rear corner where the cooker/grill and refrigerator are situated; a further hinged worktop can be seen to the side of the cooker unit. The floor in the rear kitchen section is lower than that in the main lounge/dinette section.

A close-up view of the gas cooker showing the two burners and grill.

Most elderly, coach-built motorhomes require some sort of repair and restoration, but not all quite as severe as this poor Bambi, which required a complete reroofing. This is a bird's-eye view of the interior with the roof removed.

Same roof, different angle, this is the front section over the cab.

cupboard with a hinged door, and attached to the side of the cooker unit was a hinged worktop, giving a small work area for food preparation (neatly folding against the side unit when not required). Opposite the kitchen was a sink unit with a tap and a large storage cupboard below, with an extra hinged worktop mirroring the one on the side of the cooker unit. A cleverly designed slimline wardrobe unit was incorporated into the back of the sink unit with a hinged access door. The wardrobe was deceptively spacious and contained a clothes hanging rail; the door was fitted with a vanity mirror (outside) and with an electric strip light above.

One had to step up into the lounge/dining area from the recessed floor of the kitchen, and the overall standing height within the higher level was just 5ft 3½in. This lounge/diner consisted of two long settees down each side with thick foam bases and backrests, with the settee bases offering additional storage room. An island-leg table was placed in the central isle for dining. Opening, double-glazed windows were fitted in either side of the vehicle in the lounge/diner area, and finished with fitted curtains. There was an additional surprise feature in the lounge area as the designers had incorporated room for a small chemical toilet beneath the end settee, nearest the sink, though in all likelihood this would have to be placed at the rear end of the vehicle for night use because, once the settees became a double bed, access to the toilet would not have been possible. Above the side windows were small pelmets with retaining edges running from the eye-level rear cupboards to further storage lockers (at roof height) at the front end of the living area. Spot lamps were fitted to the side of each front locker of the swivel-head variety, ideally placed for bedtime reading.

The over-cab section in the Bambi was suitable for one child to sleep in as it measured only 5ft × 2ft 4in, with a narrow window fitted with curtains. The settees in the lounge/diner had the option of being two single beds (6ft × 1ft 10in) or one double (6ft × 5ft 2½in). There were options for a second child's bed and an adult (rollaway) bunk, though within the confines of a Bambi this was possibly wishful thinking and there were probably few buyers to take

Water ingress in older motorhomes can cause major problems if left unattended, and the Bambi models are no exception. Thankfully, Tim Thornbury, who operates bedfordrascal.com, has the necessary skills to repair, rebuild and restore the majority of problems encountered on Rascal camper vans and motorhomes; his handiwork is seen in this series of pictures.

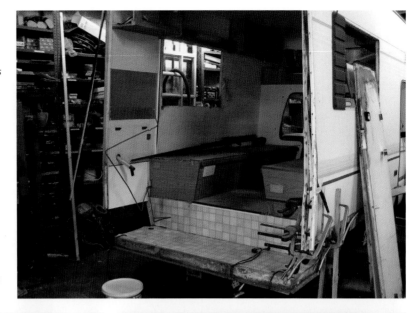

BELOW: *Tim is also called upon to repair the main Rascal cab area from time to time when the old tin worm begins to bite. The wheel arch has been replaced here.*

 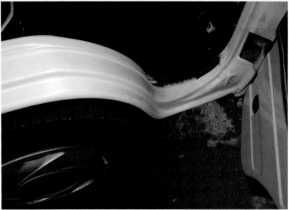

up this option. Other finishing touches in the Bambi interior included fitted carpet to the lounge/dining area floor, with vinyl fitted in the recessed end-section floor. A roof light/vent (with fly-screen) was fitted in the roof and two electric strip lights in the living area for use at night. Furniture was of a wood-grain plywood nature. An underfloor, 11gal freshwater tank was installed, and water was delivered to the sink by an electric pump. There were also two external storage lockers located on each side of the vehicle (lower front), one of which was for the spare wheel and the other for the battery, and perhaps also the hook-up cable/tools.

The buyer could choose from a long list of optional extras, including:

- heavy-duty battery
- electrical control panel and battery charger (with leisure battery)
- mains electric hook-up with twin earth leakage and overload circuit breakers
- blown-air heating with thermostat

- flushing chemical toilet
- waste-water tank
- water heater
- top-hung double-glazed windows, blinds and flyscreens
- side windows with sliding panels, blinds and flyscreens
- two forward-facing rear seats
- free-standing rear awning
- child's over-cab bed mattress
- second child's 'slide-out' bed or adult rollaway bunk
- rear corner steadies
- roof rack and detachable ladder
- bed extension to increase one bed to 7ft 9in overall
- optional waste-water tank below floor.

Autohomes' sales slogan for the new Bambi was, 'A new motor caravan for the price of a used one', and to some extent this was true as the price of a standard Bambi in the summer of 1986 was just £7,495. Autohomes ran into financial difficulties during the early 1990s, bringing to an end production

of the Bambi, but by this point around 1,500 had been produced. Many of those are still in use today and support for the Autohomes Bambi remains as strong as ever with the owners' club, which Autohomes chairman Ian Mac-pherson helped to establish in 1988 and is still going strong (2009). Spares for the Bedford Rascal currently remain available, which means that the Bambi should be around for some years to come.

I must say a special word of thanks at this stage to the Bedford Rascal restorer (and saviour of many models) Tim Thornbury of Wiltshire. Tim has operated a Bedford Rascal parts and restoration business for some years and, in the process, has carried out many repairs and complete refurbishments to the Bambi and other Rascal-based campers. Thankfully, Tim has kept a photographic record of his numerous repairs and has kindly allowed me to use a large number of his pictures in the Bedford Rascal chapters.

Elddis Nipper (Rascal)

Rear shot of the Elddis Nipper shows the rear-entry door of the stable design, split into two, allowing the top to be opened independently of the bottom section.

ABOVE LEFT: The Elddis Nipper at a quick glance could be mistaken for the Autohomes Bambi, but a closer look will reveal that the Nipper has a stepped-up section to the front roof line.
ABOVE RIGHT: This side profile of the Nipper demonstrates the roof line difference far more clearly.

At first glance, the Elddis Nipper appears to be identical to the Autohomes Bambi, but a closer inspection of the external bodywork reveals subtle differences. The Nipper, built by Elddis of Consett, County Durham, was based on the Bedford Rascal pick-up base and featured a miniature coach-built body, similar to that of the Autohomes Bambi. The major exterior difference between the Nipper and the Bambi was the top roof line, as the Nipper has a slightly raised rear section. The Elddis Nipper was obviously marketed as a direct competitor with the Bambi, in a sector that also included the Romahome, based upon the Honda/Rascal/Suzuki vehicle. An Elddis sales slogan of the time stated, 'Compare it with the competition and you'll see how much more you get for your money with the Elddis Nipper'.

Even the Nipper interior had an almost identical layout to that found in the Bambi, with a rear entrance door of the stable-type, glazed top and bottom, and the lower recessed floor area at the rear. The kitchen area had the Bambi-style layout and featured the gas hob/grill in the right corner with cutlery drawer and refrigerator beneath, storage locker at eye-level and a hinged

Interior view of the Nipper with a similar layout to the Bambi model, with the kitchen in the rear corners and lounge seats/double bed in the main area.

worktop to the side of the cooker. In the opposite corner was the sink with a storage cupboard below and a wardrobe behind with a vanity mirror on the external door and another hinged worktop to the side of the sink. Here was the first major internal difference between the Nipper and the Bambi, since the Nipper had an extra wardrobe situated alongside the corner one. The addition of a second wardrobe in the internal confines of a very small coach-built model was certainly a big sales attraction, and quite a plus point to score over its rival the Bambi. The standing height was 6ft 4in in the lower kitchen area to the rear.

On stepping up into the main lounge, one had two long settees down the sides of the vehicle, well upholstered with backrests. Whereas the Bambi had an island-leg table in the centre gangway, the designers of the Nipper had set the dining area to one side. The long settee behind the passenger cab seat formed two single (forward and rearward) seats for dining, with a table erected at meal times, thus leaving the central gangway clear and the whole of the other settee opposite free. This was a clever design idea and did, indeed, leave the whole floor space free from obstruction, and it also meant that, if only one occupant were dining, the other could still stretch out on the long settee opposite, though there was still the option of having this table in the gangway to seat four. A standard feature of the Nipper was the ability to transform both long settees into two, single, forward-facing seats when travelling, and both of these were fitted with lap retaining safety belts (early models had only one). At night the two settees could be used as either two long, single beds or one large double by utilizing the upholstered backrests, and, because the bed did not take up the whole of the floor space at the rear end, access to the chemical toilet under the settee nearest the sink was still possible. On either side of the vehicle (above the long settees) were double-glazed windows of the opening variety and, just above these, on either side was a narrow storage shelf.

At the front of the interior were two storage cupboards (one on either side of the over-cab), positioned at roof height, with reading (spot) lamps fitted

A closer view of the rear kitchen area with the sink to the left and the cooker on the right; the hinged worktops on each side of the units are again similar to the Bambi's.

A closer view of the sink unit; the wardrobe can be seen behind, with the door ajar.

A two-burner gas hob/grill combination in the rear corner with storage above.

to both bases. A mattress was supplied as standard in the over-cab area, so it was possible for a child to sleep there; this measured 5ft 3in × 2ft 5in. Other standard features of the Elddis Nipper were: fresh- and waste-water tanks fitted under the floor, a fire extinguisher and blanket in the kitchen area and rear (wind-down) corner steadies. The Nipper had external storage lockers running the length of the coach-built bodywork. These lockers (on each side) gave access to the battery, spare wheel and fuel filler; they could also house such items as the mains electric hook-up cable and other camping gear. The exterior dimensions of the Nipper were: length 12ft 1in, width 5ft 10in and overall height 8ft 2½in. The cost of an Elddis Nipper (in standard form) was £8,710 in December 1988.

In the wardrobe department the Elddis Nipper goes one better than the Bambi, as there are two of them, seen here with the doors open.

ABOVE AND RIGHT: There is excellent storage beneath the Bambi main body, with these hinged lids giving access to the gas cylinder and good storage facilities for the electric cable, for instance. The Autohomes Bambi has similar storage beneath the body.

26

Romahome (Rascal)

The Romahome demountable unit based on the Bedford Rascal remains a popular model many years after it was conceived, with an all-fibreglass body rust is not a problem. This example completed a 16,000-miles charity run without any mishaps.

The Romahome living unit can be demounted in minutes from the Rascal and left parked up on site by use of support legs.

The Romahome model, built by Island Plastics Ltd on the Isle of Wight, was the first of the micro-coach-built campers and was originally based on the little Honda Acty-van. As the name of the company implies, the Romahome was an all-fibreglass body that had an over-cab area and single entrance rear door. The Romahome became a huge sales success for the company when first released on the Honda base vehicle, so it was hardly surprising that they should use the Bedford Rascal pick-up when it was released. Until the release of the Autohomes Bambi and the Elddis Nipper, the Romahome had filled a niche market, and this continued because of a unique advantage that it had over its competitors – the Romahome was a demountable unit. This did, of course, mean that buyers of the Bedford Romahome were buying a dual-purpose vehicle, capable of being a flat-bed pick-up during the week and a camper van at weekends (the demounting process took around 15min using specialist jacks). Island Plastics were quick to point out another advantage of the demountable Romahome body in their literature:

for the private user though, that same facility of being able to detach the mechanicals from the living quarters has another connotation, which is drastically reducing the cost of replacement when a decision to change is made. Essentially, the caravan unit itself has a potential for a long usable original life, whereas the base vehicle might be

The Romahome becomes a Bedford Rascal flat-bed pick-up once the Romahome body is removed.

replaced every few years, and Island Plastics have one customer who is now on their third vehicle to carry their original Romahome body!

How right that statement has proved to be, since many Romahome models that were based on the Rascal (and, indeed, on the earlier Honda) are still in use today, often on modern micro pick-ups such as the Daihatsu Hi-jet and the Suzuki.

By the time that the Romahome was selling well on the Bedford Rascal base in 1987 a new, more streamlined shape had been created, which improved the internal space slightly. Although more refined, the basic layout remained close

to that of the original. Entry was by a single (stable-type) rear door, which was glazed top and bottom, and, once inside, one found the kitchen facilities located in each rear corner. To the right was a two-burner gas hob with grill and refrigerator (optional) below. To the side of the cooker was a hinged worktop, extending partly over the settee, and above the cooker was a storage cupboard with hinged door. In the opposite corner was the sink, fitted with a tap, with a storage cupboard below this, to the side of the sink was a further hinged (or clip-on) worktop, and above the sink was another storage cupboard with hinged door. There was full standing room in this kitchen area at the rear.

The interior of the Romahome, with a layout similar to that in both the Bambi and the Nipper, with the kitchen at the rear end and the lounge/dinette in the main body.

A close-up shot of the Romahome cooker and refrigerator situated to the right of the rear door.

On stepping up into the lounge area there were long settees down either side (both 6ft in length), well upholstered with backrests. Below these settees was a freshwater storage tank, room for the optional chemical toilet and plenty of space in which to store general camping gear. For dining, a table was clipped to the front bulkhead and supported by a folding leg at the other end. Both body sides were fitted with large, top-hinged windows (double-glazed), and a small storage pelmet ran along both sides of the vehicle above these windows. An opening roof vent was fitted in the centre of the roof, in the lounge area, and two single spot lamps were positioned at the ends of the storage pelmet.

At night the two settees in the lounge area would convert into a double bed measuring 4ft 7in × 6ft 1in, and two very small children could sleep in the over-cab area. Other interior fitments included curtains to windows and electric (12V) lights. Optional extras for the Bedford Romahome included a refrigerator, a mains electric hook-up, a leisure battery, a fire extinguisher, a chemical toilet, a window to front the over-cab area, free-standing awning, extra roof vent, warm-air heating, roller blinds and fly-screens. A Bedford Rascal Romahome had a list price of £9,187 in February 1989 for the 2/4-berth model. The Romahome body, complete with rear door and side windows, could also be purchased separately, enabling the buyer to carry out his own internal fitting-out.

The total length of a Romahome (Bedford Rascal-based) was 12ft 7½in, the overall height 7ft ¾in and the width 5ft 6½in.

ABOVE: The plastic sink is seen here to the left of the rear door, with a storage cupboard below.

RIGHT: Another view of the rear interior corner; the sink unit with its cover in place and a further storage locker can be seen above.

more *Bedford Rascal* campers

Here is the Ritz, a compact motorhome based on the Bedford Rascal chassis and built by Minilux Motorvans of Wigan. Entry is by a side door toward the rear; this model featured side collision beams in the frame, reclining cab seats and a king-size double bed.

The most popular camper van models based on the small Bedford Rascal base are those already described – the Auto-homes Bambi, the Danbury Renegade, the Elddis Nipper and the Island Plastics Romahome; these were the clear market leaders in the Rascal market, but there were others that were manu-factured in smaller numbers. In this chapter I focus upon two more Rascal-based campers.

MINILUX RITZ

One of the most intriguing of these was the Ritz Motorhome, built by Minilux Motorvans of Standish, Lancashire, and based on the Rascal pick-up. I have to admit that I stumbled upon this unusu-al model when sorting through some old sales brochures that someone had kindly given to me. It is a model that I have never actually seen, and subse-quent research has failed to discover the Ritz listed in any buyers' guides. No

one I have spoken to in the industry could remember it, nor, indeed, had ever heard of it, so I suspect that very few were ever produced, but a photo-graph at least proves that it did exist.

The Ritz was a coach-built model, which used a mixture of aluminium and GRP panels for the construction and featured a side-door entrance toward the rear. The Ritz had a striking appearance and does give the impres-sion that it was well constructed. The living area had one single double-glazed window to either side, another window in the front of the over-cab section and yet another in the rear end. The entrance door was of the stable type, split into two with a double-glazed window set in the top half.

Unfortunately the sales brochure for it contained only an exterior picture of the Ritz, so I therefore have no idea what the internal layout was like, a great pity as that side-entrance door throws up some intriguing possibilities. What I do

know for sure is that the Ritz was well equipped in its standard form and con-tained the following fitments: a large sink, two-burner hob/grill, luxury trim facings, wine-glass rack, two electric strip lights, roof vent, mountings for lap belts in the two rear seats, three-way seating system, in-built towbar, full height wardrobe, fully insulated body-work, twin dining tables, fresh- and waste-water tanks, refrigerator, rear cor-ner steadies, external lockers, reclining cab seats and a leisure battery. The list of optional extras was quite comprehen-sive and customers could add such items as a shower tray, blown-air heating system, alloy wheels, flyscreens to all windows, an opening sunroof, chemical toilet, nudge bar, extractor fan in the kitchen and, to cap it all, a colour co-ordi-nated camping trailer. The Ritz really does appear to have been quite an inter-esting little package built into the Bed-ford Rascal and one can only wonder why these models did not appear in any

The Gleneagles 5 Bedford Rascal camper van, a compact, two-berth model, which retained the original metal factory-fitted roof; built by Auto Caravan Company of Perthshire, it had a price tag of £8,837 in 1989. A high-top model on the Rascal was also available from the company.

The Gleneagles had a well designed and constructed interior, with a gas hob/grill located in the unit seen here and a sink opposite. Both the units had a hinged, single dining table at each end, which can be seen here all ready for use.

The two single seats in the rear could be turned around in order to face the tables for dining and for relaxation.

volume. The Bedford Ritz literature gives no indication of the list price, and perhaps this helps to explain its low sales, as, given the number of its standard features, it may have been priced too high, given the Rascal camper competition at the time.

The builders of the Rascal Ritz certainly took safety very seriously as reflected in their sales material:

> Totally new thinking and design has [sic] produced a mini motorhome with 3-way seating – use it like a car for travel, a bunk to snooze on, or recline fully both sides for a super king size bed measuring 6ft 4in × 5ft 3in. A lightweight but immensely strong steel frame has been evolved especially for the Ritz to ensure occupant protection and provide the security for the anchorages for seat belts which are a fundamental part of the Ritz design.

GLENEAGLES

Gleneagles campers were built in Scotland by the Auto Caravan Company of Windsole, Perthshire and produced a number of examples on different chassis, one of which included the Bedford Rascal. During the late 1980s they offered two models on the Rascal base, the Gleneagles 5, a weekender model without a rising roof, and the Gleneagles H5, which was a high-top example. Just because this conversion was based on the diminutive Rascal van, one would be quite wrong to assume that the interior was nothing but basic. Gleneagles models in general were fitted out to a high standard, and the conversion on the Rascal was no exception, with the builders not content to simply fit a cooker and sink of tiny proportions into plywood boxes.

Designing and fitting a usable interior layout in to the Bedford Rascal dimensions must have stretched the imagination of camper van designers around the country. The team at Auto Caravan must have burnt the midnight oil when configuring the internal layout for their Gleneagles model, but it certainly paid off for they produced a delightful living area in the tiny Rascal. The one-piece, rear tailgate was lifted to reveal furniture on either side of the rear, with a gas hob built into the right-hand side cupboard and a sink fitted

The two seats arranged in their forward-facing travelling position; note that no seat belts were fitted.

A view of the Gleneagles interior with the rear tailgate raised; the units to each side were built to a high standard and contained good storage space in the cupboards below the kitchen appliances.

LEFT: *Having covered the three most popular coach-built models that were produced on the Bedford Rascal base, namely the Bambi, Nipper and Romahome, it would be remiss not to include a couple of pictures of another, quite rare Rascal example, the Dalesman Dandy. It was built in a similar style to the Bambi and the Nipper with an over-cab section and a single rear door of the stable type.*

BELOW LEFT: *Rear view of the Dalesman Dandy.*
BELOW: *This was constructed in the traditional coach-built manner with aluminium profile edging covering all joints and plastic infill.*

into a cupboard on the left. These cupboards were constructed from wood and both units had ample storage space below; a single electric strip light was fitted above the sink area. Forward of these units were two single seats, one on either side, directly behind the cab seats. For daytime travel these seats were left in the forward-facing position, but for dining the seats were designed to turn around and face the rear. The designers had come up with the clever idea of mounting lift-up flaps at either end of the two kitchen units; these were secured in position for dining to act as two small tables.

Few examples of the Gleneagles Rascal have survived, but I am grateful again to Tim Thornbury who supplied the Gleneagles pictures, taken when he carried out a complete restoration on a model. As an example of price, the Gleneagles two-berth (factory roof) had a list price of £8,837 in February 1989, while the Gleneagles high-top model was priced at £9,669 in the same period.

A very neat-looking camper van, this is the Drivelodge Bijou, a rising-roof model with a modern interior; this example had passed through the workshops of Tim Thornbury at bedfordrascal.com.

RIGHT: Interior view of the Bedford Bijou model, stylish and modern white units in a U shape around the rear.

BELOW LEFT: The settee formed the double bed with the aid of a slide-out section, though floor space was very restricted once the bed was completed, as seen here through the side door.

BELOW RIGHT: The Bijou furniture was constructed from plastic-coated ply panels with a grey edging, practical and functional as well as being easy to clean. The Bedford Rascal wheel arch has been disguised by being boxed in, and above this can be seen the lift-up flap extension.

The famous Vauxhall Motors griffin logo entered the present century world of motorcaravanning on the front grille of the Vauxhall Vivaro. The beautiful silver example seen here is a high-quality camper van conversion by Concept Multi-Car Ltd of Hythe in Kent, the Vauxhall Toscana.

Vivaro Toscana: the griffin badge enters the twenty-first century

AN OVERVIEW OF THE VIVARO

In order to bring the Bedford camper van story full circle I felt that it was only fitting that a modern example which still carries the famous griffin grille badge should appear in a book covering the history of Vauxhall Motors and their long involvement with motorcaravans.

The motor industry around the world has evolved over a long period, a story of buy-outs and partnerships between some of the great vehicle marques. Vauxhall did, of course, feature in such a deal as early as the mid 1920s when they became a wholly owned subsidiary of General Motors, and by 1931 the first Bedford commercial had been produced. There was little change for the Bedford marque until the 1980s when it became IBC Vehicles, and the partnership with Isuzu, which brought us the Midi and Rascal vans. That period really did mark the end of the Bedford name as an individual brand, though it would live on as the 'B' in IBC Vehicles. In 1996 General Motors and Renault signed an agreement to produce a medium-sized van at the Luton plant and by 2001 the Vauxhall Vivaro had arrived. Motoring aficionados might argue that it was not a 'true' Vauxhall van, but that argument could be laid at the door of many models throughout motoring history. It is true that the Vivaro body shell is also available as the Renault Trafic and the Nissan Primastar, but, whatever argument

one makes, the Vivaro carries the griffin badge and is produced at the home of the Bedford marque, Luton. When most of the giant Luton-based Vauxhall car plant was demolished, the old AA factory block remained – the place where so many Bedford CFs and Rascals were assembled is the line that produces the Vivaro, thus retaining the Bedford-Vivaro link with motorcaravans.

The Vivaro became a huge success story, and by 2003 had won the award for 'Best Small Van' as voted for by *Commercial and Fleet World*; in 2006 the 400,000th Vivaro rolled off the Luton production line, once more scooping a major award, this time as *Professional Van and Truck*'s 'Van of the Year'. It would be unfair not to mention the larger Vauxhall Movano van, a commercial of bigger proportions offering full standing height and also available as the Renault Master. For some reason, the Movano was overlooked by the motorcaravan converters, a great pity as the internal load area did lend itself as an excellent base for conversion to camper van. Despite this, a couple of converters did see the Movano as an ideal camper base, one of the best being the conversion by JC Leisure in 2000. The Movano has been used on many occasions by enthusiasts of self-build models, and some excellent, well-planned motorcaravans have been built by those with the necessary skills.

Yet, despite its massive production figures and awards, one has to say that

it has been largely overlooked as a base for camper van conversion. The Vivaro was, and still is, a very good looking vehicle, well styled externally and easy to drive, with a good area to the rear with numerous camper conversion possibilities. It has been used mainly by customers requiring a bespoke (custom) conversion, and such models have been produced by several converters in Britain. One company who were wise to the qualities offered by the Vivaro was Concept Multi-Car, of Hythe, Kent (sometimes referred to as CMC Reimo); they produced the well-crafted Toscana Vivaro Sportive. CMC also introduced the German Reimo products (motorcaravan fitments) into Britain in the 1980s.

VIVARO TOSCANA

The Vivaro Toscana Sportive model produced by CMC is based on the SWB Vivaro and is a panel-van conversion with elevating (rear-hinged) roof. Extremely sporty and sleek looking, the Toscana has a single, one-piece tailgate fitted with heated rear window and wash-wipe, together with a side (sliding) entrance door fitted with a bonded sliding window. The low-line roof, which is rear hinged, rises majestically above the vehicle and remains in the upright position with the aid of gas-filled support struts at either side (an insulated high top was an option).

Internally the Toscana has a classic Volkswagen layout with furniture along

The Toscana makes use of the renowned German Reimo products, and the result is a state of the art modern camper with a sleek interior. The rear tailgate is raised here showing the fitments along the right-hand side and the rear seat/double bed laid out flat. This seat is fitted into runners mounted on the floor, allowing the seat to be moved in the interior to suit the occupants.

The interior of the Toscana as seen through the side-entry door, with seat in the travelling position (with seat belts) and the table holder located beneath the seat base.

LEFT: Like its smaller counterpart the Vivaro, the Vauxhall Movano has also been overlooked for motorhome conversion, except for those converted on a bespoke basis for individual customers. The high-top Movano has good internal space, as can be seen here on this well built example (converter unknown).

one side, and a double (bench-style) seat, which folds flat to form a double bed; and although that basic description may sound vague, the interior itself is anything but. Built with German-designed components and technology, the Toscana interior is the epitome of quality in every detail. Viewed from the side door, the Toscana had neat, grey-faced units running the full length of the interior, from just behind the driver's seat to the rear end of the vehicle. The facilities consisted of a Smev two-burner hob with mini-grill and sink, all topped off with a glass hinged top. A 50ltr compressor refrigerator completed the kitchen hardware, and a series of useful storage lockers were built into the kitchen base unit. A side window (sliding variety) was situated just above the kitchen base unit and an electric light was fitted above that. Alongside the kitchen unit was a full height storage cupboard, the front of

which had two small access doors and a large wardrobe door.

Anti-slip vinyl covered the whole floor area, and built into this were two parallel runners on which the rear seat was fixed. The crash-tested (to European safety standards) '333' seat was fitted with two three-point integral seat belts and, due to the fitment of the floor runners, had the ability to be moved along the vehicle, and, with the two cab seats turned around to face the rear, a dinette for four people was readily available. The seat (in two pieces) was folded flat at night to create a double bed measuring 6ft 5in × 4ft. Fitted to the base of the rear seat was a tubular metal table holder, and once the supporting pole of the table was fitted to this, it was possible to have either a two-person dining position or one for four, with the rear seat moved forward toward the two swivel cab seats.

Optional extras on the Toscana included a bed in the roof, a Propex heating system, a Eberspacher heater and a hot water system. Standard Vivaro features included a leather-bound steering wheel, air conditioning, electrically operated cab windows, electric door mirrors (also heated), metallic paint finish and a remote intruder alarm system. All of which is a far cry from the days of the Bedford CA and CF models.

As an example (in May 2009), and to summarize, the Toscana based on the SWB chassis 2.0 CDTi 16v (115 PS) was £30,445.93 and the SWB 2.5 CDTi 16v (146PS) was £31,857.69. The gearbox was of the six-speed variety with an optional Techshift (auto) available for an extra £940.

I offer my sincere thanks to Hilary Shortland, of Concept Multi-Car for assisting me with information and pictures of the Vivaro Toscana.

Despite the popularity of the Vivaro as a delivery vehicle, few converters have offered the vehicle as a base for camper vans. The model on view here is the high-top Highlander by Mill Garage of Duns, Berwickshire.

External view of the Highlander conversion by Mill Garage on the Vauxhall Movano.

Auto-Roam Auto-Roamer (CF)

Auto-Sleeper Bedford CF Auto-Sleeper B40, B41, B42, SB43, SB44 and SB45, CB22 (CF), SV100 (CF), Clubman (CF), Utopian SB45 (CF), Utopian CX200 (CF)

Autotrail Comanche (CF)

Bedmobile Bedmobile (CA)

Bob Spencer Motorhomes Sightseer (CF)

British Motor Caravan Company Princess (CF)

Calthorpe Home-Cruiser (CA)

Canterbury Seeker, Sunhome and Sun-liner (CF)

Caravans International Motorised (CI/M) [CI Autohomes from 1972] Brigand (CF), Bedouin Mk.I and Mk.II (CF), Autohome (CF), Motorhome (CF), Travelhome S (CF), Trailblazer (CF), Bambi (Rascal), Midihome (Midi)

Carawagon International Carawagon Express (CF)

Cavalier Coachman Cirrus, Coachman, Cumulus, Stratus (CF)

Central Car & Caravans Highlander (CA)

Cooper & Griffin Ltd Inca (CF)

Concept Multi-Car Toscana (Vauxhall Vivaro)

Compass Caravans Clipper, Drifter (CF)

Corvesgate Coachcraft Corvesgate (CF)

Cotswold Cotswold (Bedford Duple coach)

Creightons (Nelson) Ltd Creighton Clubman (CF)

CRV International Ltd Suncruiser (CF), Dreamliner (CF)

Dalesman Dalesman (CF)

Danbury Renegade, Fun Camper (Rascal)

Daytona Motorhomes Daytona B6 (CF), Daytona B4 (KB26)

Devon Dove and Domino (Midi)

Dormobile Dormobile Caravan (CA), Romany(CA), Deauville (CA), Debonair (CA), Romany II (CF), Debonair II (CF), Freeway (CF), Deauville (CF), Land Cruiser (CF)

Eagle Motorhomes Bedford Swinger (CF)

Elddis Nipper (Rascal)

European Caravans Advantura (CF), Tourstar (CF), Sundowner (CF)

Elvee Motorhomes El-Vee Grandee (CF)

Foster & Day Horizon 1350, 1600 and 1800, Arran, Shetland and Harris (CF)

Foxon Conversions Foxon (CF)

Glendale Motorhomes (previously KJ Caravans) Glendale 1000L, 2000L, 2500L, 3000L, Major, Compact (CF) and Minimotorhome (KB26)

Glevum Motor Caravans Cheltenham Olympian (CF) and Cheltenham Imperial (CF)

GT Motorised Florida, Orlando, Pompano and Tampa (CF)

Hadrian Hadrian (CA)

Holdsworth Holdsworth Standard, Super, Show-Stopper, Ranger (CF)

Howard-Lange Howard-Lange (CF)

Hymer Hymer (German import: CF/Opel Blitz)

Invincible Compact 4 (CF)

Island Plastics Romahome (Rascal)

JC Leisure Movano (Vauxhall Movano)

Jennings Roadranger and ERF Road-ranger (CF)

Jurgens Jurgens Autovilla (South African import: CF)

Kenex Carefree (CA)

Manchester Motorcaravan Co. Cara-home (CF)

Margrove Motorhomes Montrose (CF)

Mill Garage Highlander (Vivaro/Movano)

Minilux Motorvans Minilux Rascal Ritz (Rascal)

Motor Bodies Ltd Challenger (CF)

Motorhomes International (Spacemaker Group) Buccaneer and Motorsleeper (CF)

Motorsleepers Motorsleeper (CF)

Multi-Cruiser Multi-Cruiser (CF) demountable unit

Newlander Newlander (CF)

Nimbus Nimrod (CF)

Nomadic Wheels Ltd (Murvi) Mondo C, Executive Custom, Mondo S, Executive Super, Mondo S+ (CF)

North East Motorhomes Monte Cristo (CF)

Oxley Coachcraft Richmond and Blenheim (CF)

Pegasus Tourers (later: Tredigan Ltd) Pegasus (CA)

Pioneer Recreational Vehicles Pioneer (CF)

Richard Smith & Father Worcester (CF)

Ridsdale Nomad (CA)

Riverside Riverside (CF) and Riverside compact (Bedford KB26)

Transworld Bandit (CF)

Walker (later: Island Plastics) Sun-trekker (CF) demountable unit

Webster Webster Bedford (CA)

Welch & Co. Bristolian (CF)

Westbrook Motorhomes Ltd Trafford (CF)

Westcraft Motorhomes Westcraft (CF) demountable unit

York Motor Caravan Co. York (CF)

This list represents the major converters only, as listed in many motoring publications of the time. Not included are those models that were custom-built by small converters and coachbuilders in very small numbers and bespoke (custom) models to customers' own specification.

Bedford time-line

The production camper van that brought motorcaravanning to the masses in Britain, the Dormobile Caravan by Martin Walter Ltd. The Bedford CA introduction in 1952 saw the Folkestone firm invent the Bedford Dormobile, a utility van with seats that could be transformed into a bed at night. By the mid 1950s the first fully equipped Dormobile CA with rising roof had been introduced, and the rest, as the saying goes, is history.

1857 Alexander Wilson sets up Vauxhall Iron Works in London

1903 The first Vauxhall car is produced

1905 Vauxhall factory moves to the Luton site

1907 Vauxhall Motors Ltd is formed

1925 Vauxhall becomes a wholly-owned subsidiary of General Motors

1931 Vauxhall's first commercial Bedford is launched

1932 Bedford 30 and 12cwt vans introduced

1933 Bedford 3-ton truck and 8cwt van introduced

1937 Bedford sales reach 30,000 units a year

1938 Bedford 5/6cwt van introduced

1939 Bedford 10/12cwt van launched

1939–45 Vauxhall Motors become heavily involved in war-time production, which includes the building of 250,000 Bedford trucks and 5,640 Churchill tanks

1946 Peace-time vehicle production resumes at Luton. K, M and O model Bedfords go into production

1947 500,000th Bedford truck produced

1950 Bedford S-type truck and 10-ton tractor units introduced

1952 Bedford CA van launched, birth of the Bedford Dormobile

1953 Bedford A-type replaces K, M and O range

1954 £36 million expansion of the Luton plant is announced

1955 Bedford truck production moved to Dunstable

1957 Bedford 6-ton D and C models launched

1958 The one-millionth Bedford is produced; 15cwt version of the Bedford CA is introduced in January

1959 In June a 102in wheelbase version is added to the CA range, designated as the CALV; the standard CAV van is redesignated as the CASV; CA

range front end is also restyled and a one-piece windscreen fitted

1960 Bedford TK introduced; in excess of 103,000 Bedford vehicles produced, with 50,000 going for export

1961 In June a Perkins diesel engine, 4.99, becomes an option on the CA range

1964 Bedford 8cwt HA van introduced; modifications to the CA range include a bigger windscreen, restyled front grille, dashboard layout and other refinements/improvements

1965 In May a Perkins 4.108V engine becomes an option on the CA range

1969 The two-millionth Bedford is produced (in all forms); the CA range is discontinued after 370,000 were built; the Bedford CF range is introduced

1970 Bedford M-type 4×4 introduced

1972 Petrol engine sizes uprated on the CF range to 1759cc and 2279cc and a new CF variant becomes available, the 35cwt chassis-cab

1974 Bedford TM range introduced
1975 Bedford vehicles being built or assembled in twenty countries
1976 Bedford Chevanne launched
1977 GM diesel unit of 2064cc introduced to replace the Perkins option
1978 The one-millionth Bedford van and the two-millionth Bedford truck are produced
1980 Bedford TL truck introduced; Bedford CF range is given a facelift and designations of CF230, CF250, CF280 and CF350
1981 Fiftieth anniversary of Bedford models
1982 The 1.5-millionth Bedford to be exported
1983 Bedford, by this time part of the GM Overseas Commercial Vehicle Corporation, becomes the Bedford Commercial Vehicle Division
1984 The CF range now becomes the CF2, and only one petrol engine is fitted, the 1979cc; CF2 now fitted with front disc brakes; 4×4 version and electric versions of the CF2 also released
1986 GM Europe established; production of the Bedford Rascal and Midi starts
1987 Production of the CF range ends; Bedford trucks division sold to David J. Brown and new company AWD Trucks formed
1994 Production of the Midi range ends
1995 Vauxhall celebrate ninety years in Luton
1997 Vauxhall Arena van goes on sale
1996 GM and Renault reach agreement to produce a medium-sized van

at Luton; GM announce that it is to expand the IBC Vehicle plant in Luton in order to build 60,000 vans a year
1998 IBC Vehicles becomes a subsidiary of GM and a dedicated commercial vehicle plant
1999 Movano van launched
2000 Announcement that IBC Vehicles are to produce a new van; Vauxhall announce restructuring of manufacturing facilities with production of cars to cease at Luton; David Jones, designer of the famous Bedford CA, dies aged 90 (Vauxhall's director of styling 1934–71)
2001 Vivaro van in production at Luton
2003 Vivaro wins 'Best Small Van' award for second year in the *Commercial Fleet World* honours
2006 400,0000th X-83 van (Vivaro/Trafic/Primastar) built at Luton

ABOVE: *The Vauxhall Motors–Dormobile liaison went from strength to strength throughout the 1960s and Dormobile built on their sales success once the CF range was released in 1969. The Romany II, Debonair II, Contessa, Freeway, Land Cruiser and the Calypso (seen here) models were all popular examples produced at the Tile Kiln Lane plant.*

LEFT: *The Bedford CF became one of the most popular camper van and motorhome base vehicles of the 1970s, with all the major British converters offering their own configuration, one such model was the Sunhome by Canterbury seen here.*

ABOVE: Custom vans were much in vogue during the 1970s and the 1980s, and the Bedford CF van was a perfect base vehicle, and probably the most popular. The example seen here is 'Terry's All Gold' customized by the conversion specialist Terry Acreman.

RIGHT: After being in production since 1969, the CF range was finally phased out in 1987 and its replacement, the Bedford Midi, had by then been launched. A joint venture between Vauxhall and Isuzu (IBC Vehicles), the new Midi did not enjoy the same success in the motorcaravan world as a base for conversion. A high-top camper van model is seen here, the Dorset Traveller (not a model that appeared in any buyers' guides).

LEFT: Launched around the same time as the Midi van was the Bedford Rascal, and who would have thought that such a diminutive vehicle would enjoy such a sales success as a base for a camper van and motorhome conversion? The Rascal has as many fans today as it had in the 1980s and the early 1990s; prices for used Bambi, Nipper and Romahome models remain buoyant on the used/classic scene.

BELOW: The famous Vauxhall Motors/Bedford griffin badge has gone through many changes over the years; the full line-up is pictured here.

The Griffin Through The Ages

1920's 1930's 1940's 1960's 1970's 1980's 1990's 2003 2008

further reading

R. Berry and A. Earnshaw, *Bedford Light Commercials of the 1950s and 60s* **(Trans-Pennine Publishing, 2000)**
A very informative paperback written by two respected Vauxhall historians. Uses many black-and-white pictures from the Vauxhall Heritage archives and is predominantly based on the Bedford CA range. An inexpensive book, yet excellent value and one that the Bedford enthusiast should have on his bookshelf.

R. Cook, *Vauxhall: a History* **(Tempus Publishing, 2005)**
An excellent book dedicated to the history of Vauxhall Motors. Features a well-researched text about the Vauxhall cars and Bedford commercials, together with many period photographs. The story covers the history of the marque from the Vauxhall Iron Works through to the end of Vauxhall car production in Luton.

J. Hanson, *The Story of the Motor Caravan* **(Malvern House Publications, 1997)**
The smallest of all the books mentioned here, this was produced in A5 format in the style of a booklet. The northern-based transport historian John Hanson is a dedicated enthusiast of vintage, veteran and classic motorcaravans and owns several examples himself. Although small in size, this book contains many excellent photographs, a large proportion of which were published in it for the first time.

J. Hunt, *The Practical Motorcaravanner* **(David & Charles, 1983)**
Written by one of the most respected motorcaravan journalists in the country, the late John Hunt. Hunt introduced the first British monthly magazine for motorcaravanners in 1966. Many models were altered by the conversion company after he had road-tested the prototype and pointed out its shortcomings. This book was a guide to motorcaravanning on its publication and makes reference to many of the models and base vehicles of the classic period. A real 'must have' title for any classic motorcaravan enthusiast.

S. Lyons, *Motorcaravanning at Home and Abroad* **(Yeoman Publications, 1973)**
This book is really more of a 'how to' publication. It contains few or no photographs, but instead relies completely on cartoon drawings by 'Nardi' and features many humorous camping moments.

H. Myhill, *Motor Caravanning* **(Ward Locke, 1976)**
Written by a long-time motorcaravanner, who, incidentally, lived in a BMC Bluebird Highwayman for several years. Although written as a guide for motorcaravanners of the period, it is now of interest to classic camper enthusiasts simply because of the models mentioned in the text and the accompanying photographs.

C. Park, *The Complete Book of Motorcaravanning* **(Haynes, 1979)**
An excellent large format book, which was a guide to the motorcaravans of the time of its publication and is now especially interesting to classic camper enthusiasts because of the models featured.

K. Trant, *Home away from Home* **(Black Dog Publishing, 2006)**
Despite being the largest book of all those included here, it is a curious publication as it does not easily fall into a specific category. It is certainly not a guidebook for motorcaravanners, but more of a reference work that takes a look at owners and their campers, both in Britain and the USA. Although aimed heavily at the American market, it does include many British-based owners describing their campers and why they enjoy using them. It was perhaps compiled as an exercise in getting under the skin of motorhome folk in order to discover what draws them to this hugely popular pastime.

M. Watts, *Classic Camper Vans – the Inside Story* **(The Crowood Press, 2007)**
This book takes an in-depth look at all the most popular British camper vans and motorhomes built between 1956 and 1979. It covers the history of camper vans in Britain and includes a full calendar of the events during that period. It uses a good mixture of pictures to illustrate the many models and includes period brochure covers and advertisements. It also has a section featuring some weird and wonderful models. A 'must have' book for any classic camper van owner or enthusiast, with an excellent array of Bedford-based examples.

M. Watts, *Classic Dormobile Camper Vans – Products of Martin Walter Ltd and Dormobile* **(The Crowood Press, 2009)**
A title dedicated to the camper vans and motorhomes produced by Martin Walter Ltd/Dormobile at their Folkestone factory in Kent. Today the word Dormobile has become synonymous with camper vans from a bygone era, and in this title the author looks in detail at every camper van model produced at Folkestone from the 1950s through to the early 1990s. The book is packed with colour photographs, period advertisements and examples of original sales brochures.

W.M. Whiteman, *The History of the Caravan* **(Blandford Press, 1973)**
Highly regarded as one of the best books written on the subject of caravanning history. Whiteman was the founder of the Caravan Council in 1939 and editor of *Caravan* magazine for twenty-two years. This book, as the title suggests, is mainly concerned with touring/trailer caravans, but it does have a section about camper vans and includes two pictures of early Dormobile models. An interesting read for anyone with an interest in the British caravan industry and the development of touring caravans.

T. Wilkinson, *Motor Caravanning*
(David & Charles, 1968)
This book contains some interesting model profiles, line drawings and excellent photographs. Written as a guide for the period, it now represents a good source of reference for classic camper van followers.

N. Wilson, *Gypsies and Gentlemen*
(Columbus Books, 1986)
Not of great interest to classic enthusiasts, but a fascinating book for anyone interested in the development of caravanning, camping and motorcaravanning. A good historical book tracing the camping culture from early horse-drawn wagons through to the motorhomes that Viscount Montgomery used during the Second World War.

owner's clubs & useful contacts

OWNERS' CLUBS AND ASSOCIATIONS

Autohomes Owners Association
(all models converted by Autohomes of Poole)
c/o Peter Wright, 22 Boyntons, Nettlesworth,
Chester-le-Street, County Durham DH2 3PD

Auto-Sleeper Owners Club
(all Auto-Sleeper models)
Auto-Sleeper Owners Club Secretary,
Orchard Works, Willersey, nr Broadway,
Worcestershire WR12 7QF

Bambi Owners Club
(all Bambi models built by Autohomes)
www.bambiownersclub.com

Bedford-CF Club (all Bedford CF vehicles)
www.bedford-cf.co.uk

Bedford Owners Club International
(all Bedford vehicles)
27 Northville Drive, Westcliff-on Sea, Essex SS0 0QA

Bedford-World (all Bedford vehicles)
www.bedford-world.com

Classic Camper Club
(all classic camper vans built before 1988)
30 Fairwater Crescent, Alcester, Warwickshire B49 6RB

Dormobile Owners Club
(all camper vans/motorhomes
built by Martin Walter/Dormobile)
67 Upper Shelton Road, Marston Moretaine,
Bedfordshire MK43 0LU

Elddis Owners Club
(all Elddis caravans and campers,
including the Elddis Nipper)
John Harrison, 9 Brookside Avenue, Bedale,
North Yorkshire DL8 2DP

Glendale Club (all Glendale motorhomes)
c/o 4 North Place, North Terrace, Mildenhall,
Suffolk IP28 7AB

Holdsworth Owners Club (all conversions by
Holdsworth)
C. Chamberlain, 14 Barracks Lane, Shirehapton,
Bristol BS11 9NG

Period Motor Caravan Guild
(all motorcaravans built before 1973)
J. Hanson, 116 Copgrove Road, Leeds LS8 2RS

Self-Build Motor Caravan Club
(specialist club catering for all self-built campers)
www.sbmcc.co.uk

Vauxhall Viva Owners Club
(all Viva models, including the HA-based camper vans)
c/o 2 Bracken Way, Newport, Shropshire TF10 7RL

SPECIALIST PARTS SUPPLIERS

Adrian Bailey Classics
(specialist supplier of Bedford CF parts, new and used)
www.roverland.eu
0113 263 4288

Bedford Rascal Specialist
(all things connected with the Bedford Rascal, including
spares, repairs, restoration and conversion)
www.bedfordrascal.com
01249 721350

Classic Vauxhall Services
(Bedford CA parts, service, repair and restoration)
Canal Bridge Works, Byfleet Road,
New Haw, Surrey KT15 3JE
01932 845858

Powertrack
(brake specialist, covers all
models from 1935 to 1980)
www.powertrack.co.uk
01753 842680

Smith and Deakin
(fibreglass wings and bonnets for the Bedford CF)
Unit 75, Blackpole Trading Estate, Worcester WR3 8TJ
www.smithanddeakin.co.uk
01905 458886

Speedy Spares
(supplier of classic vehicle parts/spares,
including Bedford)
19–25 Old Shoreham Road, Portslade-by-Sea,
East Sussex BN41 1SP
www.speedyspares.co.uk
01273 417889

index